winning
running

winning running

Bill Dellinger
with George Beres

cbi Contemporary Books, Inc.
Chicago

Dedicated to the men of Oregon

Published by Contemporary Books, Inc.
180 North Michigan Avenue, Chicago, Illinois 60601
Manufactured in the United States of America
Library of Congress Catalog Card Number: 77-91152
International Standard Book Number: 0-8092-7673-9 (cloth)
                                     0-8092-7672-0 (paper)

Published simultaneously in Canada by
Beaverbooks
953 Dillingham Road
Pickering, Ontario L1W 1Z7
Canada

contents

acknowledgments

Russ Werner and Bill Bowerman, my coaches, for inspiration and knowledge of track and field.

Dr. Eugene Evonuk, physiologist, University of Oregon, whose advice and consultation I sought in writing this book.

introduction

Running is the oldest of competitive sports. Countless generations have shared the running experience, putting one stride after the other to reach the finish line.

Old though it may be, the sport of running still is breaking new ground. Each succeeding generation of runners has been bigger, stronger, and physiologically more capable of improving upon existing standards.

In addition, the modern runner has the advantage of technological and medical advances that have made possible athletic achievements once considered beyond the reach of man.

But the true key to an individual runner's progress remains unchanged: the ability of teacher/coach to communicate running knowledge to him, combined with his own ability to absorb and make use of this knowledge.

Experience is the ultimate teacher. But much valuable time is squandered when a runner—trusting only in his own experience—takes many wrong "turns" while seeking the best route on his own. It is the experience of others that can serve as signposts for him along the way. The transmitting of that knowledge from a veteran runner or a coach can save an inexperienced runner many fruitless trips down "dead ends."

Good advice, based on modern training principles, is the surest way for a runner to perform at the maximum of his abilities without wasted motions or effort.

It is my hope that this book—based on procedures and instincts developed at Oregon—will help you to get the most from distance running, both in achievement and enjoyment. The techniques described have led runners of all types and capabilities to great success at Oregon. They can do the same for you.

winning
running

chapter one

a runner's philosophy

A runner's philosophy is subject to many of the same influences that affect other areas of life around us. It has to be in tune with the technical and scientific developments of modern life.

That is especially true of the distance runner, whose competitive life may cover a period as long as two decades. He has to be willing to adapt to the rapid advances in training and competitive techniques. He can learn from coaches, from his fellow runners, and from his own experiences. But he always should be ready to experiment.

At Oregon we have a tradition of running built around the approach to the sport of two of the great innovators of track history, coaches Bill Hayward and Bill Bowerman. We have to acknowledge that everything from technology to vitamin supplements has broadened the performance potential of the distance runner beyond what it was in their coaching days. But some principles remain—as they were under the Haywards and Bowermans—the foundation for the development of the individual runner.

These are the fundamentals that still serve as guideposts for the runner who hopes not only to keep pace but to set the pace.

PRINCIPLE ONE: MODERATION

Even good things in excess can become harmful. If a college runner shows a 10 percent improvement each year and leaves school with an appetite for more competition, he has made positive progress. The best years for competition should be somewhere between the ages of 24 and 32. Unfortunately, many fine high school and college runners are so misused by their school coaches that they leave the program no longer looking forward to training or hungry for competition. In many cases they have chronic injuries that rule out further competition.

In September 1963, I decided to make a comeback after a three-year layoff. My goal was to make our Olympic team in the 5,000 meters for the Tokyo Olympics of 1964. The popular concept at that time was that running 120 miles a week was the key to success. I started out on a 120-mile-a-week program and lasted about eight weeks. Even though I was tired, I found myself running 17 miles a day, simply to get in my mileage. I eventually reached a point where I was unable to train because of illness brought on by continued fatigue.

I found out the hard way that pure mileage for mileage's sake was not the answer. If 120 miles a week was the secret to running, we all would be victorious runners!

Moderation should apply to all facets of the runner's life. He should enjoy the "good things" of life, but with moderation. Too often a program is built on negatives (don't stay out late, don't have a social life) to the point where running takes on a negative connotation. Running and competing are not ends in themselves, but means to an end. I tell runners: "Let common sense rule; use moderation."

PRINCIPLE TWO: PROGRESSION

At Oregon, the runner's program begins in the middle of August with progression pointed toward a peaking in performance sometime the following June or July, depending on the individual's ability. The individual's progression can be controlled by what I call "date pace" and "goal pace." In most cases, the toughest part of training is holding back so that you will not peak too soon. That's where date pace and goal pace fit in.

In establishing a goal pace, a runner must consider his experience and competitive records. I ask each runner his goal for the year. In many cases we compromise between what he thinks he is capable of doing and my evaluation of his ability. The establishing of the runner's goal in running for the year is done on an individual basis in the privacy of the track office or at home.

I vividly remember my talk with Steve Prefontaine when he entered Oregon as a freshman. When I asked him his goal in the mile for his freshman year, he replied, "3:48.0"! At that time he was a 4:06 high school miler. Needless to say, I liked the confidence he had, but managed to convince him that he was expecting too much for a one-year jump. Through compromise we ended up with a goal of 3:56 for his freshman year. He ended the season running 3:57.1!

Establishing the date pace for each runner is a more objective procedure. Sometime during the first three weeks of school in the fall each runner is asked to run his distance at a pace that is comfortable for him. I do not give him splits on this trial run, as I do not want to influence his pace. The time he runs for this trial becomes his date pace for his primary event.

With date and goal pace established, each runner can plot his own progress on a chart.

3

Name: **MATT CENTROWITZ**   OREGON TRACK   Event: **MILE**   Goal: **3:54**

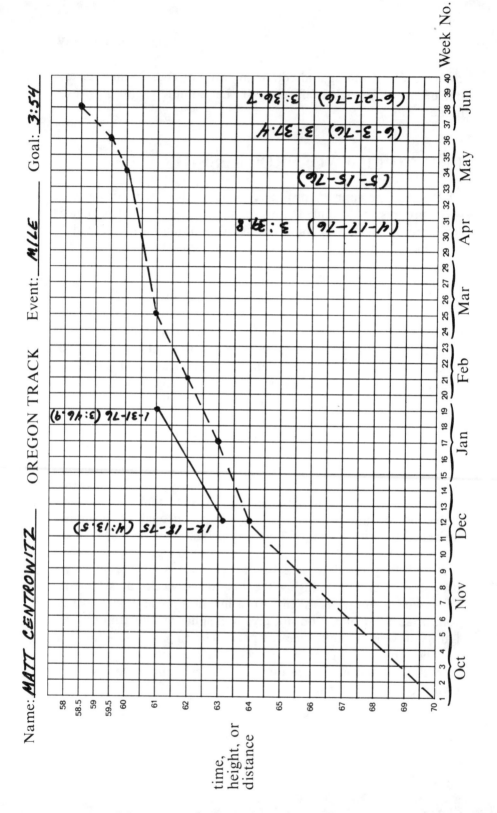

Week No.

time,
height, or
distance

In a goal oriented and date pace program, it is necessary to evaluate the progress of the individual runner. A runner can be tested approximately every three weeks during the noncompetitive season. He should always test at 3/4 effort of date pace in an attempt to hold back. During this period of training and testing, he must be ready for any change. That brings us to a third principle.

PRINCIPLE THREE: ADAPTABILITY

One of the ingredients of a sound running program is the ability of the coach to adapt his program to the particular situation he faces. If he has been a good teacher, his pupils will acquire this ability and demonstrate it on their own in later years of competition or coaching.

Good common sense is needed in adapting a running program for each individual, reflecting many variables. Weather, terrain, facilities, health of the individual, and many other unforeseen circumstances will truly test one's ingenuity as a runner.

In 1957, I was in the air force and stationed at a remote radar site on the northern tip of the Olympic peninsula in Washington. It was 80 miles to the nearest town that had a track. So I had to adapt. I developed a method of doing intervals on the beach by counting my strides. I would count to myself each time my right foot touched down until I reached ten. I would then put one finger out to keep track. I would continue this process for the equivalent of 12 fingers, estimating this to be approximately a 440. I would run up and down this stretch of beach doing 220's, 330's, 440's, 660's, 880's, and 1320's by what I call the "count system." I used this system for eight months of training without ever stepping onto a track, never knowing exactly how far I was running or how fast. The first time I stepped onto a track the following spring for a test effort, I ran a solo 4:05 mile! I went on that year to set American records in the 1,500-meter, 2-mile, 3-mile, and 5,000-meters. To this day, as a jogger, I find myself occasionally counting to myself as my right foot touches down.

Incidentally, I found when I got onto the track that it took me only ten fingers and two strides to run a 60-second 440, six fingers for a 32-second 220.

I had to adapt in that instance to environment and terrain. I could tell many similar stories of adapting running programs for various other reasons. The point is that to be successful you must be willing to adapt, be flexible and bend a little. Anyone who outlines a weekly program and carries it through rigidly without this consideration is in trouble. It is because of this principle that I refuse to coach a runner by correspondence. I believe personal contact is necessary to be able to adapt the program to meet the requirements of the individual by taking into consideration all the various conditions.

PRINCIPLE FOUR: VARIATION

A runner should continually seek variations in the running program. Your attitude toward running is directly affected by this principle. It is boring to know that on Monday you will be running 440's, Tuesday a 3/4-mile time trial, Wednesday 330's, etc.

An important reason for varying a program is to meet individual needs. Interval running ought to be based on date progression and individual goal pace, which will vary for each individual's workout on the track.

Not only do workouts vary from individual to individual, but the same workout seldom is given twice. It is healthy to vary the pattern of running, not anticipating what is coming up the next week. Variation leads to mental freshness. With variety in running patterns, the runner is more likely to look forward to the training necessary for him to reach his full potential.

There are other ways of varying a program to keep it interesting, challenging, and meaningful. Vary the area or terrain. Work at higher elevations, on country roads, in city parks, on golf courses. Runners can benefit from changing their running partners—a good way to get to know all their team-mates.

Variation in climate is important in a running program. We all know there is little we can do about the weather. There are advantages to running in areas such as Oregon, where there is a wide range of weather conducive to a good running program.

PRINCIPLE FIVE: CALLOUSING EFFECT

If using a pick and shovel is a new experience for you, there will be a period of adjusting to soreness and blisters before you develop the callouses that make it possible to handle those tools efficiently and without undue stress. This callousing effect also applies to running. It is not always possible to anticipate all the stresses or unknown circumstances that can arise in a competitive situation. But you can try. The runner constantly should try to add to his practice routine situations designed to "callous" himself.

I keep referring to myself in examples. That's natural for any coach, since he has his own experiences to offer a runner. In some cases, the developing runner's experiences come the hard way, by personal trial and error. In others, they come the smart way—through the knowledge of others.

In 1956, I decided (with urging from my coach, Bill Bowerman) to run the 5,000 meters rather than the 1,500 in our Olympic tryouts. I had won the NCAA Championship in the mile in 1954, and was the runner-up to a classmate, Jim Bailey, in 1955. The mile was my favorite race, but I had to agree with Bowerman that I had a better chance of making our team in the 5,000. But what a callousing effect! That first 5,000 I ran in competition was the longest, hardest race I had ever run, simply because I was not calloused for that distance at that pace. I developed a severe stitch on the tenth lap and wasn't too sure I could finish.

In 1956, during the Olympic games in Melbourne, Australia, I had the opportunity to watch one of the greatest 10,000-meter races of all time. Two of the participants in that race, Vladimir Kuts and Gordon Pirie, had traded off beating each other and setting world records at 5,000 meters. In their last meeting prior to the Olympics, Gordon had defeated Vladimir by sitting on him, letting him do all the work, then out-sprinting him at the end. Pirie had boasted he would use the same tactic in beating Vladimir for the Olympic title in the 10,000. What he didn't know was that Kuts was callousing himself to an uneven style of running, while Pirie was training on even pace, the acceptable method at that time. Vladimir led Pirie and the rest of the 10,000 field through a 59-second first lap! He continued that suicide pace for a 1:59 first 800 meters. At this time he was leading, with Pirie one-half stride behind and the rest of the field some 70 yards back. Then Vladimir began throwing in the varied pace he had calloused himself to. He would sprint the straightaways and jog the turns for a few laps, then he threw in a few laps of running a 220 in around 28 with a rest of 42 for the next 220. Three different times the 5'7" Vladimir turned around and motioned to the 6'2" Gordon Pirie to pass him. Each time Gordon shook his head, "No." With four laps to go in this 25-lap race, Vladimir moved out to the second lane and stopped! Pirie either had to pass him or stop with him and let the rest of the field catch them. He went by Vladimir, who immediately fell in behind him for about 20 yards and then sprinted by him. This time Gordon let him go! Vladimir ended the race, arm raised, fist clenched to the roar of the crowd; Gordon finished jogging in, the rest of the field having caught and passed him. This is a prime example of the importance of the callousing effect. Gordon Pirie was easily the second-best runner in the 10,000-meter field—perhaps the best, except that he had attempted a style of running he was unprepared for.

Murray Halberg won the 5,000 in the 1960 Rome Olympics by putting in a 58-second lap with three to go. He opened up a 40-yard lead and was able to hang on for the victory. Again, this just didn't happen by chance, but was well planned and prepared for. Tactics are important considerations in preparing runners. A runner must callous himself in practice for the tactic he wishes to employ in a competitive situation. If the opponent has not used the tactic, it becomes an effective weapon.

Equally important is being calloused to weather conditions, patterns of competition, terrain, time of day, type of track, and many other factors that may influence how one competes.

If a runner in the national championship has preliminaries on Thursday, semifinals on Friday, and finals on Saturday, this schedule should be simulated in several practice sessions several weeks in advance of the championships to callous him to this pattern.

If the national cross-country championship is being conducted on a course with a lot of hills, the runners should be challenged with this type of terrain in several workouts prior to the competition.

If the championship is conducted at 11 A.M. and the runner is not accustomed or calloused to hard running that early, it can become a disadvantage.

Weather can be a tough one to simulate in a practice situation. If one is to acclimate to altitude, it takes approximately six to eight weeks of training at altitude. If one is to prepare himself for heat and humidity, two to three weeks are the minimum. It's tough to simulate altitude if you live in Kansas. It's tough to simulate heat and humidity if you live in the Pacific Northwest.

In 1974, the NCAA Championships were in Austin, Texas. We knew we'd be facing a heat and humidity situation. Physiologically speaking, the problem a runner confronts in heat and humidity is that his perspiration does not evaporate on the skin surface, and he is thus deprived of the cooling effect for surface blood. Without this cooling effect, the core temperature will rise. This is dangerous, possibly fatal, to the runner.

Using the advice of a local physiologist we attempted to callous our runners by working them out during the hottest part of the day while they wore their sweats. The idea was that the sweats would prevent the evaporation of perspiration, thus simulating the humidity effect. One problem: We never had a day above 60° F. in the two weeks prior to the NCAA

Championships. Needless to say, our runners suffered in the 90° F. heat and 80+ humidity in Texas, and they turned in sub-par performances.

As the running programs are presented in the following chapters, an attempt will be made to point out various callousing procedures used and how various running principles apply.

A program that fits the individual provides for enjoyment in training and eagerness for competition, and helps promote self-confidence.

chapter two

a brief history— and modern trends in running

In using the phrase "modern trends in running," I refer to the period from the early 1950s to the present. Although great advances have been made in track and field in the past 30 years, most running programs still are based on interval training, Fartlek training, or a combination of both.

The advantages of a controlled interval program were popularized by the German coach, Woldeman Gerschler. Running greats, Rudolf Harbig, Jose Barthel, Roger Moens, Gordon Pirie, and others thrived on training schedules based on individually programmed intervals—the slow scientific building of physiological and psychological resistance to stress.

Franz Stampfl refined the interval system, stressing a year-round training program and the inexorable reduction in time of intervals. Through his system, the first sub-four-minute mile was run by Roger Bannister in 1954.

Mihalz Igloi, the great Hungarian coach, whose runners at one time in the middle 1950s held every world record from 1,000 meters through 20 kilometers, used an interval program. Igloi's approach emphasized quality and intensity of work rather than duration and quantity. Jim Grelle, who trained under Igloi for five years, told me that at the end of a two-hour workout, Mihalz asked him and Jim Beatty to run an all-out 440! They both broke 50 seconds, and were amazed they could run that fast at the end of an intense two-hour session of intervals.

Two sessions of training a day have done for running what weight lifting has done for the weight events in track and field. I realize there have been some individual runners who have experimented with double sessions of training. However, if credit should go to one man for this improvement, it should go to Igloi. During the mid-1950s his pupils engaged in as many as 700 separate training sessions in a single year, necessitating two and three-a-day workouts.

Equally successful and popular at this time was the Fartlek system. It emerged from the pattern of delightful, exhausting runs through the pine forests of Sweden which produced the liquid, smooth-running machines known as Kalarue, Haag, Anderson, Strand, Ahlden, Albertson, and Gustavsson. Coaches Ernie Hjertberg and Geosta Holmer became known as fathers of the Fartlek system. Fartlek is a Swedish term meaning "speed play." This system employed all facets of the actual race. Pace striding, sprinting, jogging, and even walking were incorporated.

In the early 1960s, Arthur Lydiard introduced to the track world his system of Fartlek training now called "Lydiard Fartlek." Through such track greats as Murray Halberg, Peter Snell, and Bill Baillie, his system became universally known and accepted. His system involves a steady, rather than varied, run for a certain measured distance or time. It was devised by necessity, as he had to tend a shoe store at this time and could not spend hours with his runners on the track.

Although the United States enjoyed huge success in most

areas of track and field during this time, the runners and running programs suffered. We had an occasional breakthrough such as Horace Ashenfelter winning the steeplechase in the 1948 Olympics. But, for the most part, our runners were considered second-rate, and they were not invited to compete on the European circuit.

In 1956, I won our Olympic tryouts in the 5,000 meters, setting a new American record of 14:26. When I arrived at Melbourne, Australia, for the Olympic Games, I was shocked to discover the extensive training employed by runners from the rest of the world. Mine had consisted of cross-country running in the fall, an occasional run during the winter months, a lot of handball and other recreational types of sports. I did not begin a structured daily training program until early March. I found that my competitors in Melbourne not only trained year-round, but were training twice a day. No wonder my time of 14:26 was almost a full minute behind the then world record of 13:35! That was a time I felt was impossible to run. I also discovered that at age 21, I was the youngest of the runners in the 5,000 finals. Vladimir Kuts, the winner, was 27!

The eight-year span from the '56 Olympics to the '64 Tokyo Olympics was a time of drastic changes and tremendous improvements in our running programs. We began training year-round. We used two-a-day training sessions. We continued to train and compete after completing college. Certainly the United States had an abundance of running talent. But we lacked the know-how and programs that offered an opportunity to train and compete once out of our school systems.

The year 1958 brought the first of our great international competitions with the Russians. Our runners for the first time were given the opportunity to travel on the European continent and compete against the best. The value of what we learned about foreign training programs was inestimable. Many new ideas for training were brought back, given to our coaches, and incorporated into our programs. We discovered that our bodies not only would stand stresses put on them by vigorous year-round training, but became stronger because of it. In the '64

Olympics, American runners were first and third in the 5,000, first and ninth in the 10,000, and fourth in the steeplechase. Suddenly the American runners began to be taken seriously and considered threats by foreign runners.

With great improvements being made by adding stress to our training programs, it became popular to "stack on" mileage. Gerry Lindgren, the high school phenomenon in the middle 1960s, was running 120 miles a week, with an occasional 50-mile training session in a single day. There were rumors that some of the foreigh runners were up to 250 miles a week in their training. Suddenly, achieving excellence meant running had to become a full-time occupation. Some runners were training three and four sessions a day in an attempt to get in the mileage. The average individual with family and job responsibilities was finding it very difficult. Many were asking if it really was worth it.

It took but a few years to find that although runners were achieving almost immediate improvement, it was a mixed blessing. The runners who were on the high-mileage programs began to have problems. They could not sustain this quantity over a period of time without breaking down physically.

Misinformed, uninformed, and—in some unfortunate cases—greedy coaches looking to build a reputation pushed runners to the breaking point. They reinforced the misconceptions of runners who believed mileage was the secret to success. This led to many running-related injuries, a subject that will be covered in a later chapter.

The many injuries, fatigue factors, and psychological problems associated with the overload principle in running have resulted, fortunately, in the trend back to moderation in training, with quantity and quality being blended into successful programs.

Although we closed the international gap and became competitive through the 1960s and into the early 1970s, foreign runners now again are enjoying an advantage. We are far behind our friends overseas in terms of utilizing scientific research related to running and in involving our physicians and physiologists in our programs.

Through a muscle biopsy, a physiologist can identify muscle fiber types, telling us the percentage of speed, strength, and endurance components. With this information we could establish specificity of exercise training related to these muscle fiber types. For instance, a runner possessing muscle fibers of 60 percent speed component could be placed on a program to better develop and exploit his speed.

Biochemical techniques also can enable us to better understand our nutritional needs in regard to specificity of exercise.

The measurement of maximum oxygen intake and cardiac output—and their relationship to various exercises and training regimens—is used in many countries to direct sports activists into areas best suited to their talents. How many Steve Prefontaines or Frank Shorters have gone through our educational programs without being discovered?

The above procedures require the cooperation of physicians and physiologists. I believe that in some of the countries taking advantage of this multidiscipline approach, the sports population (activists) has a greater appreciation for physiological function as related to performance. This in turn becomes a stimulus for the scientist. The governments of these countries not only encourage athletes and scientists, but support them financially!

If we are to stay with the modern trend of supplying our athletes with specificities of exercise training aimed at their individual talents, we need some programs. We need to educate our athletes on the advantages available to them through intensive medical-physiological study of their potential.

Our physicians and physiologists have the know-how and equipment. Certainly, we have the athletes!

What we need is the implementation of a program that provides this service.

chapter three

the mental approach to training and competition

Many physiologists estimate that 80 percent of the total performance capabilities of an individual is genetically endowed. Through proper training it would be expected that an individual would achieve this 80 percent and exceed it to a point approaching his total capacity: his genetic endowment plus the training effect.

A prime example of genetic endowment would be the Kenyans, who are now very prominent in and, in many cases, dominate our collegiate and international scene of distance running. For generations, walking and running have been their mode of transportation. Many of them have been running two to ten miles daily since childhood—and at altitudes of 6,000 to 8,000 feet. Now, through the availability to them of structured programs in American universities, we witness the results of the training when applied to their endowed talent.

We all have varying levels of endowed running talent. It is through proper training that we become able to approach our total capacity. Now to some rather subjective factors I believe to be important in accomplishing total capacity.

SELF-DISCIPLINE

One of the qualities which sets one man apart from another is the variation in the amount of self-discipline. While we have limitations placed on our endowed talents, there is no such limitation on this quality.

It can be developed to such a point where it becomes a determining factor in an event. I have seen many examples of an athlete with less innate talent training to reach his total capacity and defeating athletes of superior talent, but who never reached their total capacity because of lack of self-discipline.

Lars Kaupang, a Norwegian student, came to Oregon as a 4:17 miler. My evaluation of Lars, based on four years of working with him as an undergraduate student at Oregon, is that he had a great capacity for self-discipline and a normal share of endowed talent. His improvement in running was gradual but steady. He graduated from Oregon a sub-four-minute miler. For the past two seasons at home in Norway he has been their national 1,500-meter champion. With his capacity for discipline, I feel confident Lars will continue to improve. I couldn't try to judge what his ultimate total capacity would be!

Developing self-discipline depends on a realization of its importance early in one's life. Accepting disciplines imposed by parents is invaluable in later years, when one has to generate self-discipline. One needs no special talent, advanced education, "luck," or superior intellect to discipline oneself more effectively with each passing day. One needs only the resolute determination to do so!

MENTAL TOUGHNESS

Mental toughness is a relative term, often used but seldom defined. Simply put, it is found in one who competes to the best of his ability regardless of the circumstances. He may not always win his event. But if he has performed to his total capacity, regardless of the conditions, he is a champion in my book.

I believe a good running program should develop mental toughness. In training it emerges by occasionally challenging the runner with workouts designed to test his full capacity, physically and mentally. The training session must approach the limit, but not surpass it. Mental toughness is enhanced by accomplishment, not failure.

The easiest way is not always the best way to promote mental toughness. Primitive training facilities, adverse weather, and other obstacles can cultivate mental toughness. A runner must face tough situations in training to callous himself for tough situations in competition.

Another factor in mental toughness is what I prefer to call the "inverted pyramid" effect. The runner who has achieved success finds himself in a position where people expect him to be tough and compete well, regardless of circumstances. Because of the expectations placed upon him, he has to be tough. Steve Prefontaine told me that what his fans expected from him helped sustain him in races that were so tough he was ready to break. The runner who does not have these expectations placed upon him finds it easier to break when the pace gets tough. Once this happens, it will be easier to break the second time!

WINNING ATTITUDE

To be a winner, one must think of oneself as a winner. Self-confidence is a necessity. It can stem partly from confidence in your coach and his program. One of the greatest aids a runner can have is a coach and running program in which he has unquestionable faith. A trademark of all the great coaches is this ability to gain the respect and confidence of the men they are training.

As a person matures, he naturally gains a certain degree of confidence in himself. Experience soon teaches the runner his strengths and weaknesses. We gain confidence by doing that which we know we can do well and by avoiding that which we recognize is beyond our capabilities.

Youth does not have this advantage. To develop a winner's attitude, one should allow room for achievable success. Competitions should be fun-time activities. If the goal is to participate and to have fun, everyone can be a winner, regardless of finish.

I believe all young runners should start out as sprinters. Knowing how to sprint is a valuable weapon in later years when a runner turns to the distance events.

A structured running program should not begin until at least the junior high school years.

Do not be afraid to daydream about winning. You must picture yourself a winner. When I was training for the 1964 Tokyo Olympics, I'm sure I ran that race at least 10,000 times in my mind. Each time I ran the race it would be under different circumstances with varying conditions and tactics being thrown at me. Funny thing, I always won! But dreaming is a deadend unless it is blended with self-discipline and a willingness to punish yourself with hard work.

A program that enhances a winning attitude is one that does not put undue pressure on finishing first. It is a mistake for a coach to tell his runner that he has to win, or for the runner to put undue pressure on himself by believing he must win.

I ask my runners to compete to the best of their ability under all circumstances. Maximum effort can become a habit. Runners must have faith that their coach would not enter them in events for which they are ill-prepared. Achievement and satisfaction isn't exclusively for the runner who finishes first. It is shared by anyone who knows in his gut that he gets the maximum from his abilities.

I would not want to pinpoint the blend of ingredients for greatness. Someday we may have psychological and physiological testings even for this, because great advances are being made in both areas.

I do know I have seen greatness: In the eyes of Steve Prefontaine at the starting line; in the concentration of Mac Wilkins preparing for a discus throw; and in the stubbornness of a child at play who loses, but comes back again and again until he finally succeeds.

The path to achieving total capacity can be mapped out. Its guideposts include:

(1) Demanding and expecting discipline.

(2) Allowing for accomplishment through progression.

(3) Allowing for individual differences in training.

(4) Using common sense.

(5) Developing a callousing effect for physical progression and mental preparation.

(6) Allowing for, and utilizing, feedback from runners.

(7) Challenging oneself to the limit on occasion.

(8) Placing emphasis on participation rather than on "coming in first."

The runner can speed up his development of these qualities by:

Being patient.

Being realistic.

Being goal-oriented.

Being persistent.

Being consistent.

Using common sense.

Completing workouts, even if adjustments have to be made.

Asking questions.

Listening.

Disciplining himself in all phases of life.

chapter four

oregon running patterns— tactics and drills

CROSS-COUNTRY

One of the great appeals of cross-country is that it presents the challenge of varying terrains. It brings together the best of the milers, steeplechasers, 5,000, 10,000, and marathon runners. It provides one of the few occasions when specialists from these varied events may test each other. It is a "runner's" championship. It involves a genuine team effort in that each member of the squad is of equal importance in determining the team title.

We have been in a position of cross-country dominance at Oregon, winning four national championships, being runner-up twice, and placing third twice in the past nine years. To accomplish this we have had to have quality runners—in quantity.

The start of a championship cross-country meet,
Bloomington, Indiana.

Our cross-country season is short. We usually begin classes the
last week of September. The championships are the third week
of November.

Several years ago we divided our runners into three groups of
near equal ability. One group was put in a straight interval
program. The second went on a program combining interval and
Fartlek training. And the third went on a straight Fartlek
program. We found that the group on straight interval training
made the quickest gains in conditioning and had the best results
in the early testing. But by the end of the year this group also
had the most injuries, and found it difficult to retain its early
conditioning advantage.

Yet, because of our limited season, our fall program is heavy
on intervals that produce quick results. Once the cross-country
season is over, we return to a blend of Fartlek and interval
training for a more lasting effect.

The runners going into our structured schedule prepare for it by running 30 to 50 miles a week during the summer. As September approaches, I ask them to work up to 60 to 70 miles a week. I ask them to twice a week simulate some intervals on a golf course or other grassy area. I ask them to twice a week go on a moderately hard run covering 10 to 12 miles.

In the chapter on philosophy I spoke of several principles. In the following pages you will see these principles applied to fit our cross-country situation. The comments section will explain the whys and wherefores of the workout.

All of our runners are involved in this program, so we group them into separate categories.

Patterns presented for cross-country will show a three-week preparation prior to competition and a two-week pattern during the season.

Runners enjoying the variations in cross-country,
Tokatee Golf Course.

EVENT: 21-day preparation for cross-country

WEEK:

DATES:

DAY	WORKOUT	COMMENTS
M **1**	AM—4 to 7 miles PM—60-minute varied Fartlek run	
Tu **2**	AM—4 to 7 miles PM—(1) 4 x ¾ mile (Goal pace for 6 miles) (440 rest) 　　　(2) 3 x mile—5:00—4:48—4:32 (880 rest) 　　　(3) Light grass	
W **3**	AM—4 to 7 miles PM—5 to 10 miles steady	

Th **4**	AM—4 to 7 miles PM—(1) 9 x 330 uphill (easy—medium—hard) (2) 30-minute run	
F **5**	AM—Light run PM—Light run	

Sa **6**	10:00 AM—Simulated drill covering 10 miles
	(1) 1 x ¾—60—65—70 for 3:15
	(2) 10 miles at 6 minute pace (1 x ¾ in middle at 3:21
	     even pace)
	(3) 1 x ¾ at end of 10 miles, reversing order 70—65—
	     60	

Su **7**	12 to 15 miles easy	

EVENT:

WEEK:

DATES:

DAY	WORKOUT	COMMENTS
M **8**	AM—4 to 7 miles PM—45-minute varied Fartlek run	
Tu **9**	AM—4 to 7 miles PM—10-mile control run timing each mile—6:00 mile/5:00 mile/6:00 mile/5:00 mile/etc.	
W **10**	AM—4 to 7 miles easy PM—4 to 7 miles easy	

Th **11**	AM—4 to 7 miles PM—(1) 9 x 330 uphill (easy—medium—hard) (2) Light run	
F **12**	AM—Light run PM—Light run	

Sa
13
	10:00 AM
	6 x 1 mile cut-down (440 rest)
	    start at 5:20, making each mile faster, ending at
	    approximately 4:32	

Su **14**	12 to 15 miles easy	

EVENT:

WEEK:

DATES:

DAY	WORKOUT	COMMENTS
M **15**	AM—4 to 7 miles PM—40-minute varied Fartlek run	

Tu
 16
	AM—4 to 7 miles
	 PM—(1) 3 x ¾ mile—888—440 on grass (440 rest)
	        (Goal pace for 6 miles)
	    (2) Light grass	

W **17**	AM—4 to 7 miles PM—4 to 7 miles	

Th **18**	AM—4 to 7 miles PM—(1) 9 x 330 uphill (easy—medium—hard) (2) 30-minute easy run	
F **19**	AM—Light ·run PM—Light run	
Sa **20**	10:00 AM—Simulated drill for 10 miles (1) 1 x ¾—60—65—70 (2) 10 miles at 6:00 pace (middle ¾ mile 3:12-3:18) (3) 1 x ¾—70—65—60 at finish	
Su **21**	12 to 15 miles easy	

EVENT: 14-day competitive pattern

WEEK:

DATES:

DAY	WORKOUT	COMMENTS
M **1**	AM—4 to 7 miles PM—40-minute varied Fartlek run	
Tu **2**	AM—4-mile control run at 5:00 per mile PM—(1) 1 x mile—Goal for 10,000 meters (2) 2 x ¾—Goal for 5,000 meters (3) 3 x 880—Date pace for 1,500 (4) 4 x 440—Cut downs	
W **3**	AM—4 to 7 miles PM—7 to 10 miles at comfortable pace	

Th **4**	AM—4 to 7 miles PM—(1) 9 x 330 uphill (easy—medium—hard) (2) 30-minute run	
F **5**	AM—Light run PM—Light run	
Sa **6**	10:00 AM (1) 1 x mile—4:08—4:12 (2) 10-mile run at 6:20 pace PM—Light run	If no competition, mile should be at ¾ goal pace. 4:08-4:12 meets most of our times at Oregon.
Su **7**	12 to 15 miles comfortable	

EVENT:

WEEK:

DATES:

DAY	WORKOUT	COMMENTS
M 8	AM—5-mile control run at 5:20 per mile PM—45-minute varied Fartlek run	
Tu 9	AM—4 to 7 miles PM—(1) 1 x mile (Goal pace for 5,000) (2) 5-mile run at 6:20 pace (3) 1 x mile (Goal pace for 5,000)	
W 10	AM—4 to 7 miles PM—5 to 8 miles—steady pace	

Th 11	AM—4 to 7 miles PM—(1) 1 x ¾ (Goal for 5,000 meters) (2) 5 miles easy run (3) 3 x 330—Cut-downs	
F 12	AM—Light run PM—Light run	
Sa 13	11:00 AM COMPETITION Cross-country	
Su 14	12 to 17 easy	

Cross-Country Tactics

In cross-country there are two considerations in regard to tactics—tactics involving the individual and team tactics. Both types of tactics are important for the final results.

Individual Tactics. Everyone must compete to the best of his ability. If he is the number-one runner for his team, his goal is to be competitive with the leaders of the opposition.

Runners should be calloused to going out fast for position, sustaining a good pace, and finishing strong. This can be incorporated into workouts.

Other tactics to be considered on an individual basis are:

(1) Throw in a strong surge in the middle of the race in an attempt to break away from the pack.

(2) Learn to run at full, controllable speed downhill. Many runners will attempt to rest on the downhill portion of a race, and it is a good time to make a surprise move.

(3) Reverse the procedure and run hard up the hill and relax on the downhill portion.

(4) Callous oneself for uneven running. Crowded running conditions, hills, and sharp turns require this.

Team Tactics. Tactics involving a team effort include the following:

(1) If you are the third man on your team, pick the third man on the opposing team to key on to beat. The same is true for all team members.

(2) Running as a pack is useful in encouraging slower members of the squad to stay up front. However, this is not helpful if opposing team members are in front.

THE 800

To be a great 800-meter runner you have to have the speed of a quarter-miler and the strength of a miler. Experience, as always, helps. Because of the shortness of the race and the fact that it is

Cross-country runners at Tokatee Golf Course in Oregon.

not run in lanes throughout, tactics are critical. The talent usually prevails. Many 800-meter races have been won by the experienced runner using correct tactics against a more talented but less experienced opponent.

During the '60s and early '70s, the 800 was dominated by runners capable of running great miles. Jim Ryun and Peter Snell are examples. At one time, each of these runners held the world record in both the 800 and the mile. Wade Bell, Oregon's record holder in the 800, also was a sub-four-minute miler.

With Alberto Juantorena of Cuba dominating both the 400 and 800 meters in the 1976 Montreal Olympics, I believe we will

Mike Boit of Kenya competes in the 800 at the Prefontaine Classic.

see more quarter-milers moving up to the 800 distance and more 800-meter runners training with speed for the 400.

In our patterns for the 800 we try to exploit the individual's particular talent. If the runner shows speed over strength, he trains on a 400/800 pattern. If he favors strength, he goes on an 800/1,500 pattern.

Patterns presented here include a 21-day noncompetitive program, 14-day competitive program, and 10-day preparation for major competition for the two types of 800 men.

The comment section again details the "why" of a workout and how it relates to tactics, so important in the 800.

Randal Markey of the University of Oregon is a runner with a
range of 800-1,500.

EVENT: 800-400: 21-day noncompetitive pattern

WEEK:

DATES:

DAY	WORKOUT	COMMENTS
M **1**	PM—(1) 1 x 660 breakdown (660: 75 (440)—550: 70 (440)—440 (65)—330 (47)—220 (30)—110 (13)) (2) 20-minute grass run	
Tu **2**	PM—(1) 30-minute run (2) Weight program	
W **3**	PM—(1) 3 x 220 sets (880 rest between sets) (2) 5 x 220—33—31—29—27—25 (220 rest)	

Th **4**	PM—(1) 30-minute run (2) Weight program	
F **5**	PM—(1) 5 x 300 (Goal pace for 800) (2) 20-minute run	
Sa **6**	(1) 30-minute run (2) Weight routine	
Su **7**	5-mile run	

EVENT:

WEEK:

DATES:

DAY	WORKOUT	COMMENTS
M **8**	(1) 5 x 550 up gradual hill (2) Light run	
Tu **9**	(1) 8 x 110 (12 seconds) (110-220 rest) (2) Light run (3) Weight routine	
W **10**	5 miles steady pace	

Th 11	(1) Light run (2) Weights	

F 12	(1) 880 simulated drill #1
	(2) 4 x 165 Accelerate 55
	                Float 55
	                Accelerate 55	

Sa 13	(1) 880 simulated drill #2 (2) 5 x 300 yds.—starting at date pace—cutting each down, ending at faster than goal	
Su 14	5 miles comfortable pace	

EVENT:

WEEK:

DATES:

DAY	WORKOUT	COMMENTS
M 15	(1) 660 (70)—550 (65)—440 (60)—330 (43)—220 (26)— 　　　110 (11.5) (2) 3-mile run	
Tu 16	(1) 30-minute run (2) Weight program	
W 17	(1) 12 x 110 (12) (110—220 rest) (2) Light run	

Th **18**	(1) Simulated 800 drill #3 (2) Light run (3) 5 x 330 (cut-down from date pace)	
F **19**	(1) 3 x 440—55—53—51 (440 rest) (2) Light grass	
Sa **20**	(1) 880 test effort (date pace) (2) 5-mile run (3) 6 x 330 (start at date cut to goal) (4) Light weights	
Su **21**	5-mile run	

EVENT: 800-400: 14-day competitive pattern

WEEK:

DATES:

DAY	WORKOUT	COMMENTS
M **1**	(1) 550—330—165 (goal pace) (2) 5 x 220 (goal pace) (3) Grass run	
Tu **2**	(1) 12 x 110 (12) (110 rest) (2) Light grass (3) Weight program (light)	
W **3**	(1) 1 x 660 (goal pace for 800) (2) 5 x 300 (date cutting down to goal)	

Th **4**	(1) Light grass run (2) Weights (light work)	
F **5**	(1) Simulated 800 drill #4 (2) Light grass	
Sa **6**	COMPETITION (1) Open 400 (2) Mile relay PM—Weight routine	
Su **7**	5-mile run	

EVENT:

WEEK:

DATES:

DAY	WORKOUT	COMMENTS

M
 	
8
	(1) 660 (65)—550 (60)—440 (55)—330 (40)—220 (25)—
	      110 (11)*
	
	*Times listed are for a distance of 440 yards unless otherwise
	        indicated.
	
	(2) Light grass	

Tu **9**	(1) 3 x 165—Accelerate 55—Float 55—Accelerate 55 (2) 3 x 165—Float 55—Accelerate 55—Float 55 (3) Light grass (4) Weight routine	Simulating change of pace for tactics in 800 competition.

W
 	
10
	(1) 5 x 300—pass 220—28
	                      26
	(2) Light grass 25
	                      24
	                      23	

Th **11**	(1) Light grass run (2) Weight routine (light)	
F **12**	(1) Light grass run (2) 2 x 110 (12)	
Sa **13**	COMPETITION (1) *800* (2) *Mile relay* (if possible) PM—Weight routine	
Su **14**	(1) Simulate 800 drill #5 (2) Light grass	

EVENT: 800-400: 10-day championship pattern

WEEK:

DATES:

DAY	WORKOUT	COMMENTS
Th **1**	(1) 1 x 660 (57)—550 (55)—440 (53)—330 (38)—220 (24)—110 (11) (2) Light grass	
F **2**	11 AM—4 x 110 (11) (220 rest) PM—Light grass run	
Sa **3**	(1) 1 x 660 passing 440 (51-52) (2) 5 x 220 (24-26) (220 rest) (3) Light grass	

Su **4**	5 miles comfortable pace	
M **5**	11 AM—3 x 165 sprint—float—sprint PM—30-minute grass run	
Tu **6**	(1) 5 x 220 (25) (220 rest) (2) Light grass	
W **7**	20 to 30 minutes light grass with 2-4 x grass strides of 150 yards	

EVENT:

WEEK:

DATES:

DAY	WORKOUT	COMMENTS
Th **8**	Qualifying 800	
F **9**	Semifinals 800	
Sa **10**	Finals 800	

Matt Centrowitz wins the 1,500
in dual meet in Eugene, Oregon
(school record holder for the 1,500, 3:37.6).

EVENT: 800-1,500: 21-day noncompetitive pattern

WEEK:

DATES:

DAY	WORKOUT	COMMENTS
M **1**	AM—3 to 5 miles easy PM—(1) 40-minute varied Fartlek run (2) Weight routine	
Tu **2**	AM—3 to 5 miles PM—control 8-mile run at 5:30—6:00 per mile	Time is given at each mile marker.
W **3**	AM—3 to 5 miles PM—(1) 30 to 40 minutes at steady pace (2) Weight routine	

Th **4**	AM—3 to 5 miles PM—(1) 3 x 440 (60-52) (440 rest) (2) 30-minute run (3) 3 x 330 cut-down	Starting at 60, we attempt to get down to 52 before the season.
F **5**	AM—Light run PM—(1) Light run (2) Weight routine	
Sa **6**	AM—Light run PM—(1) Simulated 800 drill #1 (2) 5-mile run (3) 9 x 330 cut-down (110 rest)	Starting at simulated 800 drill #1 and reaching #9 before season.
Su **7**	8 to 12 miles	

EVENT:

WEEK:

DATES:

DAY	WORKOUT	COMMENTS
M **8**	AM—3 to 5 miles PM—(1) 40-minute varied Fartlek run (2) Weight routine	

Tu
 	
9
	AM—3 to 5 miles
	
	PM—(1) 440—660—440—220 (220 rest) (goal pace for
	            mile)
	     (2) 7-mile run at 5:30 per mile	

W **10**	AM—3 to 5 miles PM—(1) 7 to 10 miles at comfortable pace (2) Weight routine	

Th 11	AM—3 to 5 miles PM—5-mile run—control	Starting at 6:00 per mile and attempting 5:00 per mile before competitive season.
F 12	AM—Light run PM—(1) Light run (2) Weight routine	
Sa 13	AM—Light run PM—(1) 6 x 880—330 drill cut-down (2) Light run	We do this drill off the track on a marked off area of sawdust trail. Starting at 2:30 for the 880 and attempting to reach 2:12 by season. 330's are in 50.
Su 14	8 to 12 miles easy	

EVENT:

WEEK:

DATES:

DAY	WORKOUT	COMMENTS
M **15**	AM—3 to 5 miles PM—(1) 40-minute varied Fartlek (2) Weight routine	
Tu **16**	AM—3 to 5 miles PM—(1) Control 8-mile run (2) 6 x 330 cut-down (110 rest)	On cut-downs we start at comfortable pace, making each faster, with last one 9/10 effort.
W **17**	AM—3 to 5 miles PM—(1) 30-minute easy run (2) Weight routine	

Th **18**	AM—3 to 5 miles PM—(1) 3 x 440 (60-52) (2) 20-minute grass run (3) 3 x 330 cut-down (110 rest)	See comment, day #4.
F **19**	AM—Light grass run PM—(1) Light grass run (2) Weight routine	
Sa **20**	AM—Light run PM—(1) Mile trial (date pace) (2) 5-mile run (3) 9 x 330 cut-down	
Su **21**	8 to 12 miles comfortable pace	

EVENT: 800-1,500: 14-day competitive pattern

WEEK:

DATES:

DAY	WORKOUT	COMMENTS
M **1**	AM—3 to 5 miles PM—45-minute varied Fartlek run	
Tu **2**	AM—3 to 5 miles PM—(1) 440—660—440—220 (goal pace for mile) (2) 4 x 880—330 drill on sawdust trails (3) Light run	
W **3**	AM—3 to 5 miles PM—(1) 30 to 40-minute grass run (2) Weight routine	

Th **4**	AM—3 to 5 miles PM—(1) 3 x 175 sprint—float—sprint 　　　(2) 20-minute grass run	
F **5**	AM—3 to 5 miles PM—Simulated 800 drill	Starting at #1 and progressing through #5 by end of season.
Sa **6**	COMPETITION *800 meters* PM—Weight routine	
Su **7**	(1) Simulated 800 drill (2) Light grass run	Starting at #5 and reaching #9 by end of season.

EVENT:

WEEK:

DATES:

DAY	WORKOUT	COMMENTS
M **8**	AM—3 to 5 miles PM—(1) 40-minute varied Fartlek (2) Weight routine	
Tu **9**	AM—3 to 6 miles PM—(1) 3 x 880 goal pace for mile (440 rest) (2) 6 x 330 cut-down	
W **10**	AM—4 to 7 miles PM—(1) 4 to 7 miles steady pace (2) Weight routine	

Th **11**	AM—3 to 5 miles PM—(1) 3 x 440—(53-55) (2) Light grass run	
F **12**	AM—Light grass PM—Light grass	
Sa **13**	COMPETITION *Mile* PM—Weight routine	
Su **14**	8 to 12 miles	

EVENT: 800-1,500: 10-day championship preparation

WEEK:

DATES:

DAY	WORKOUT	COMMENTS
Th **1**	AM—Light run PM—(1) 880 or 800 time trial (full effort) (2) 30-minute grass run	
F **2**	AM—20-minute grass run 11 AM 2 x 220 (24) PM—Light grass run	
Sa **3**	AM—Light grass run PM—(1) 2½ laps/1½ laps at goal pace for mile (660 rest) (2) 5 x 330 cut-down (3) Light grass run	

Su **4**	7 to 9 miles	
M **5**	AM—3 to 5 miles 11 AM 3 x 330—40.5 (220 rest) AM—20 to 30-minute grass run	
Tu **6**	AM—3 to 5 miles PM—(1) 3 x 440—(54-56) 440 rest (2) Light grass run	
W **7**	AM—Light grass run PM—Light grass run	

EVENT:

WEEK:

DATES:

DAY	WORKOUT	COMMENTS
Th **8**	COMPETITION *1,500* or *800*	
F **9**	COMPETITION, if necessary; if not, light grass run	
Sa **10**	COMPETITION *1,500* or *800*	

Simulated Progressive Drills for the 800

Testing #1

    110—goal pace
    660—80 pace for 440
    110—goal pace

Testing #2

    110—goal pace
    220—40
    110—goal pace
    330—60
    110—goal pace

Testing #3

    220—goal pace
    440—80
    220—goal pace

Testing #4

    330—goal pace
    330—60
    220—goal pace

Testing #5

    330—goal pace
    220—45
    330—goal pace

Testing #6

    440—goal pace
    220—45
    220—goal pace

Testing #7

   220—goal pace
   220—45
   440—goal pace

Testing #8

   550—goal pace
   220—45
   110—goal pace

Testing #9

   110—goal pace
   220—45
   550—goal pace

800 Tactics

A well-prepared runner should have more than one weapon for his race plan. Many times he must wait until the race develops before deciding upon his tactics. The opponent, weather conditions, track conditions, and "feelings" will dictate which weapon to use.

The following tactical patterns are by no means complete, but they do offer a few suggestions. Obviously, not all of the tactics would be used in one race situation!

   (1) Lane one on an offset start can be a big disadvantage. As the runners come off the turn and cut for the pole, the runner in lane one can find himself boxed. To offset this, the runner in lane one should:

      (a) accelerate around the turn assuring himself the lead as he comes off the turn, or

      (b) as he comes off the turn and passes the cut line, edge his way into lane two, allowing himself the straightaway for positioning.

Rick Wohlhuter comes off the offset of the 800 and takes the lead.

(2) Accelerate the back stretch of the second lap approximately 300 yards from the finish. Relax around the turn without loss of speed. When challenged coming off the final turn, be ready to accelerate again.

(3) Learn to sprint-float-sprint for 55 yards each. This is particularly useful in your drive down the final straightaway.

(4) If following, never run directly behind another runner; position yourself just outside. When you are challenged, and passed, pass your man and fall into the same position behind the man just passing you.

Note the correct position of the second man. He is in position off the outside shoulder of the man in front.

(5) Avoid running too close to the curb; at the same time, don't leave room for an opponent to pass on your inside. It's a fine line.

(6) Accelerate into final turn; relax, but carry speed off the turn; then accelerate for the final 55 yards.

(7) If the wind is in your face down the back stretch of the final lap, allow your opponent to lead so he shields the wind.

Pass him on the turn, taking the lead into the final straightaway with the wind to your back.

(8) If the wind is in your face on the final straightaway, take the lead going into the last turn. Come on the turn in the lead, giving your opponent two challengers to meet: the wind and you!

(9) Practice one-step accelerations (165's-sprint-float-sprint). Pass your opponent, using a quick acceleration for surprise, rather than slowly passing him. Remember: Quickness comes from shortening the stride for acceleration, rather than from lengthening the stride.

THE MILE (1,500)

In a survey of fans and sportswriters conducted by *Track and Field News,* the mile (1,500) was easily the most popular race in track. The race is long enough for the fans to see the developing strategies employed by the runners, yet short enough that a mistake in tactics can be fatal.

The mile has been a popular race at Oregon in terms of spectator interest and attracting aspiring young runners throughout the country. The University of Oregon has produced 20 sub-four-minute milers! Several years ago, Bill Bowerman was asked, "What's the secret for Oregon's success in producing sub-four-minute milers?" He answered: "It must be the chromosomes in the cabbage." That answer may not be too far off. Oregon's varied weather, undulating hills, and favorable environmental conditions all are conducive to good running.

In order to be a good miler, you must have the speed to run a good 800 and the strength to move up to the 5,000 and be competitive.

In our training pattern for the mile at Oregon, we provide a range of running from the 800 through the 5,000.

Patterns for the 800 and 1,500 were presented in the section on the 800. The following patterns are for a miler with 5,000-meter potential.

EVENT: 1,500-5,000: 21-day pattern

WEEK:

DATES:

DAY	WORKOUT	COMMENTS
M 1	AM—4 to 6 miles PM—(1) 45-minute varied Fartlek run 　　　(2) 8 x 220 (30/30)	30/30 refers to a 30-second 220 with a 30-second rest.
Tu 2	AM—4 to 6 miles PM—6 x 880—330 drill 　　　(Each 880 faster, keeping the 330 constant pace, approximately 50)	This drill is on a sawdust trail. Attempt to stay off track for this drill.
W 3	AM—4 to 6 miles PM—45-minute steady run at 6:20 mile pace	

Th **4**	AM—4 to 6 miles PM—(1) 3 x 440 (60) (440 rest) (2) 30-minute run	On this workout we start somewhere around 60 in December and will be down to 53 by June.
F **5**	AM—Light run PM—Light run	
Sa **6**	AM—Light run PM—10-mile control run at 5:12—5:20 mile pace	
Su **7**	12 to 15 miles comfortable pace	

EVENT:

WEEK:

DATES:

DAY	WORKOUT	COMMENTS
M **8**	AM—4 to 6 miles PM—(1) 45-minute varied Fartlek (2) 6 x 220 (30/30)	
Tu **9**	AM—4 to 6 miles PM—10-mile control-run at 5:30—5:40 mile pace	
W **10**	AM—4 to 6 miles PM—45-minute run at comfortable steady pace	

Th **11**	AM—4 to 6 miles PM—(1) 440—660—440—220 (goal pace for mile) (2) 30-minute run at comfortable pace	
F **12**	AM—Light run (20 minutes) PM—Light run (20 to 30 minutes)	
Sa **13**	AM—Light run PM—(1) Simulated 5,000 drill #1 (2) 7-mile run at comfortable pace	
Su **14**	12 to 15 miles comfortable pace	

EVENT:

WEEK:

DATES:

DAY	WORKOUT	COMMENTS
M **15**	AM—4 to 6 miles PM—(1) 45-minute varied Fartlek run (2) 10 x 220 (30/30)	
Tu **16**	AM—4 to 6 miles PM—8-mile control run at 5-minute mile pace	
W **17**	AM—4 to 6-mile run PM—Light run	

Th **18**	AM—4 to 6 miles PM—(1) Simulated mile drill #1 (2) 30-minute run	We start with simulated drill #1 and #2 and reach #11 and #12 before competitive season.
F **19**	AM—Light run PM—Light run	

Sa
 	
20
	AM—Light run
	
	PM—(1) Simulated mile drill #2
	    (2) 20-minute easy run
	    (3) 3 x 880 cut-down (70-66-62)	

Su **21**	12 to 15 miles comfortable pace	

WEEK:

DATES:

DAY	WORKOUT	COMMENTS
M **1**	AM—3 to 7 miles PM—(1) 40-minute varied Fartlek run (2) 6-8 x 220 (30/30)	
Tu **2**	AM—3 to 7 miles PM—(1) 3 x 880 (goal pace for mile) (2) 9 x 330—(48-45-42) (110 rest) (3) Light grass	
W **3**	AM—3 to 7 miles PM—40-minute easy run	

Th **4**	AM—3 to 7 miles PM—(1) 440—660—440—220 (goal pace for mile) 　　(2) 30-minute run	
F **5**	AM—Light run PM—Light run	
Sa **6**	AM—Light grass run PM—COMPETITION	Competition could range from 800 to a 5,000. We attempt to vary the distance, depending upon the situation.
Su **7**	12-mile run	

EVENT:

WEEK:

DATES:

DAY	WORKOUT	COMMENTS
M **8**	AM—3 to 7 miles PM—(1) 45-minute varied Fartlek run 　　(2) 4 x 165—accelerate 55—float 55—accelerate 　　　　55	
Tu **9**	AM—3 to 7 miles PM—(1) 440—660—440—220 (goal pace for mile) 　　(2) 2-4 x 660 (75)—550 (70)—440 (65)—330 (45)— 　　　　220 (28)—110 (13)	
W **10**	AM—3 to 7 miles PM—5 to 7 miles comfortable pace	

Th **11**	AM—3 to 7 miles PM—(1) 3 x 440 (55) (440 rest) 　　　(2) 20-minute run 　　　(3) 3 x 330—(48-45-42)	
F **12**	AM—Light run PM—Light run	
Sa **13**	AM—Light run PM—COMPETITION	
Su **14**	8 to 12 miles	

EVENT: 1,500-5,000: 10-day pattern

WEEK:

DATES:

DAY	WORKOUT	COMMENTS
Th **1**	AM—5 to 7 miles PM—(1) 4 x 880 (goal pace plus 2 seconds per lap) (440 rest) (2) 4 x 440 (goal pace) (330 rest) (3) 4 x 220 (goal pace minus 2 seconds per 220)	
F **2**	AM—Light grass run PM—Light grass run	
Sa **3**	AM—Light grass run PM—(1) 880 trial (full effort) (2) 5 miles comfortable pace (3) 5 x 330 cut-down (110 rest)	

Su **4**	AM—Light grass run PM—Light grass run	
M **5**	AM—3 to 7 miles PM—(1) 30 minutes comfortable pace (2) 6 x 220 (30/30)	
Tu **6**	AM—3 to 6 miles PM—(1) 3 x 440 (52-54) (330 rest) (2) Light grass run	
W **7**	AM—Light grass PM—(1) Light grass run (2) 3-5 x grass strides	

EVENT:

WEEK:

DATES:

DAY	WORKOUT	COMMENTS
Th **8**	AM—Light grass run PM—COMPETITION *1,500* (qualifying round)	
F **9**	AM—Light grass run PM—Light grass if no semifinals	
Sa **10**	COMPETITION *1,500*	

Mile (1,500) Tactics

The mile is very similar to the 800 in terms of tactics. The mile, or 1,500, is becoming more and more a "sprint" race. The tactics presented for the 800 apply also to this event; they can be supplemented with these additional strategic techniques:

(1) If racing a faster opponent, start your drive for the finish 660 to 600 yards out.

(2) The race is never won in the first 220! Run your own pace for the first 220. The tendency is to go out too fast, which will put yourself into oxygen debt.

(3) Work on the third lap! The tendency is to relax on this quarter. An experienced miler can win the race by pushing the pace on this lap.

Simulated Progressive Drills for Mile (1,500)

Drill #1

1st 220—goal
3 laps—75-80
last 220—goal

Drill #2

220—goal
550—75-80
220—goal
550—75-80
220—goal

Drill #3

330—goal
2½—75-80
330—goal

Drill #4

    330—goal
    440—75-80
    220—goal
    440—75-80
    220—goal

Drill #5

    440—goal
    880—75-80
    440—goal

Drill #6

    440—goal
    330—60 (80 pace)
    220—goal
    330—60
    440—goal

Drill #7

    550—goal
    660—80 pace
    550—goal

Drill #8

    550—goal
    220—45
    220—goal
    220—45
    550—goal

Drill #9

    660—goal
    440—80-90
    660—goal

Drill #10

    880—goal
    440—80-90
    440—goal

Drill #11

    990—goal
    440—80-90
    330—goal

Drill #12

    2½—goal
    440—90
    220—goal

Drill #13

    2½—goal
    330—60-70 (80-90)
    330—goal

THE STEEPLECHASE

In some ways the steeplechase event is the stepchild of distance running in the United States. Historically, it has been an event distance men have turned to if they find they are not going to excel in the 1,500 or 5,000-meter event.

That attitude is reflected in the limited United States steeplechase achievement in international competition: Horace Ashenfelter's gold medal in the 1952 Olympics and George Young's bronze in the 1968 Olympics.

Our country is handicapped by the absence of a 2,000-meter steeplechase event in high school track. Only when we start offering our budding Prefontaines and Liquories the steeple as a primary event at the beginning levels of running will we begin to consistently produce world class steeplers.

The steeplechase is a challenging event because it requires more than pure running ability. It also demands well-developed skills.

Because of these demands—and as a result of the limited opportunity for running the steeple at the interscholastic level—the runners coming into the college programs have had virtually no experience in the event. So we have to identify steeplechase prospects by testing our runners.

Every runner coming into our program is tested by going through some preliminary steeplechase drills. Those who show promise continue progressive drills for developing their full potential as steeplers.

This section will review:

1) The Oregon testing system for selection of the best personnel for the steeplechase;

2) Our progressive drills for developing the special skills necessary for steepling;

3) Our method of preparing steeplers for competition.

An obvious prerequisite for steepling is that one be a good runner. Where can one better develop his running talent than in cross-country? So our evaluation of steeplechase personnel begins during the cross-country season in the fall.

Early in December, when cross-country ends, we have a chance to take an in-depth look at runners with steeplechasing potential. It's to a steepler's advantage to have good flexibility and agility and to be six feet tall. But height doesn't have to be a determining factor. The steeplechase champion in the 1964 Olympics stood just 5'7". Running talent and hurdle and water-jumping technique are the vital factors, regardless of the runner's size.

The first move is to acquaint your distance men with the hurdle.

STEP 1: The runner walks up to a low hurdle (30 inches high). He steps with what will be the trail leg to the side and approximately two feet back from the hurdle, letting the lead knee come up as in running form, then stepping past the hurdle and bringing the trail leg over the side. This is the same trail leg action as in hurdling. It is important for the heel to come up near the buttock and for the toe to turn out. It is equally important for the lead leg to come up bent (we call this "leading with the knee") and then to go directly at the hurdle. A runner with steeplechase potential will pick up this drill in one session.

STEP 2: The runner jogs up to the hurdle, steps over the right or left side of the hurdle, and brings the trail leg over.

STEP 3: The runner jogs up and steps directly OVER the hurdle, instead of passing it at the side as before.

STEP 4: Three hurdles are placed down the straightaway approximately 20 to 25 yards apart, with three more at the same intervals coming back the same straightaway. Our potential steeplers jog down the straightaway, going over the 30-inch hurdles with alternating lead legs. After clearing the third hurdle, they continue down the track approximately another 40 yards, then return over three more hurdles. The emphasis in this drill is not only on familiarizing the runner with hurdle tech-

In the trail leg drill, the trail leg should be lower
for correct position.

nique, but also in leading with either the right or left leg. There
is a great advantage to be gained in check mark adjustment
when the runner can accomplish this.

STEP 5: The runner follows the same turnaround drill as in
Step 4, but with the hurdles elevated to 36 inches, the same as
the actual steeple barrier.

STEP 6: This is the final step before going to hurdle intervals.
At this point the runner will learn to hit a check mark to

In the turnaround drill for hurdle technique, the hurdles are spaced 30 to 40 yards apart.

accelerate his final few strides into the barrier. We use a check mark approximately 13 yards from the barrier. The runner uses it as a guide to adjust his stride so as to hit with his lead leg. He then accelerates the next few strides to hurdle the barrier. The takeoff spot will depend largely on the speed of approach, but should fall between 5½ to six feet. A check mark will insure rhythm and proper takeoff position for each barrier. Acceleration is used to maintain forward momentum, prevent loss of speed, and avoid "sit-back" over the barrier. As the runner's foot touches the track beyond the barrier, it is essential that his center of gravity be directly over the lead leg. The runner who can lead with either leg over the barrier will have fewer difficulties adjusting to the check mark.

The steepler clears the barrier during steeplechase competition. Note that his clearance is a little high.

Acceleration into the barrier, low clearance, rhythm, balance, and relaxation are skills the steepler will develop through continued use of these drills as part of his warmup routine or in a workout.

Water Jump Progression

The water jump phase of steepling requires skill and an element of courage. The runner must charge aggressively, jump atop the three-foot high barrier, hurl himself out over the water pit, land on one leg, and continue running without loss of momentum.

It takes time and discipline to develop the skills required to efficiently clear the water hazard. Lead-up routines are the basis

The runner hits the check mark (left), then accelerates to the second mark for jumping action (right). The two shirts are actually 9 feet apart.

for developing these skills. Just as important, they develop the confidence that enables the runner to overcome any fear he might have had of the water jump.

Lead-up activities at Oregon include use of a trampoline that is a permanent drill tool kept at the track stadium. Starting in the fall, our potential steeplechasers spend 15 to 20 minutes, twice a week, on the trampoline—bouncing and going through simple stunts such as seat drops, back drops, and front drops.

While this develops balance and body awareness, it also creates leg strength. All three are elements essential for developing the skills required of a steeplechaser.

STEP 1: The runner learns to hit a check mark approximately 13 yards out; he accelerates onto a scratch made on our dirt intramural track, jumps over a water puddle (it can be an imaginary one), and continues to run. By learning to do this off either leg, he will be in a good position to develop the proper stride adjustment to the water barrier for his advanced stages of development. After two weeks of these two-a-week drills, the runner is ready for the next step.

STEP 2: A length of wood about 12 inches high is used as a launching support for a practice leap over an imaginary water pit. At Oregon we use a cut from a fir tree. The runner reaches a check mark, accelerates, steps on the wood support, and leaps to a landing approximately 10 to 12 feet out.

STEP 3: This is a duplicate of Step 2, except for the doubling of the thickness of the section of wood used for support on the leap. This raises the height to about 23 inches for drills that should continue for two to four weeks.

STEP 4: The runner now has his first encounter with the actual 36-inch steeplechase barrier. It is placed at the end of the long jump runway. The runner comes down the runway at an approximate quarter speed of 70 seconds. He hits a check mark about 13 yards out—his signal to accelerate the last few strides to the barrier. He jumps on top of the barrier, pushes out, and lands in the sand of the long jump pit. He must land on one leg and run out of the pit without breaking stride. The runner is instructed to land on top of the barrier, his toe over its edge. He is in spikes for this drill to gain the traction from the spikes catching on the front of the barrier. He must rotate over the barrier with the leg still bent before pushing out. If the runner extends his leg before his center of gravity passes over the barrier, he will leap too high, which will cost him distance over the water. We use a marker in the sand, 12 feet out, to represent the distance necessary for proper water clearance. The runner stays on this drill until he is confident of his acceleration onto

In the water-jump drill
into the long-jump pit,
the runner should stay low over the top of the barrier. He should
not extend his leg until he pushes out, not up.

This is a good example of toe-over-barrier running, pushing out rather than up for water clearance.

the barrier and until he becomes proficient at clearing the barrier with a bent leg, landing on the opposite leg, and continuing out of the pit without loss of momentum.

STEP 5: Now the runner moves to the regular water jump pit and barrier—but with one major difference: The pit is covered with plywood. So the runner at this stage lands on a flat surface without water. At this point of progression, the runner begins to get some interval work that uses hurdles and the covered water jump.

STEP 6: Here we begin a limited amount of work over the actual barriers, with the plywood cover removed and the pit filled with water. The goal at this stage is for the runner to have overcome any fear of the water jump and barriers. As for continued development of hurdling and water clearance skills— that's a long-term project that can take years.

Training Patterns for Steeplechase

Patterns of training for the steeplechase include a 21-day "off season" program, a 14-day pattern for competitive season, and a 10-day pattern in preparation for championship competition.

Steeplechase Tactics

Probably fewer tactics are involved in the steeplechase than in the flat races, because of the high degree of skill demanded by the barriers and water jumps.

Accelerating for the barrier and water jump is a challenge in itself without throwing in additional accelerations as a tactic!

In place of tactics, the following "suggestions" may help your steeplechase.

(1) In most cases you are better off to start conservatively, running in a position where you have a good view of the oncoming barrier or water jump and staying clear of a tightly grouped pack of runners. If necessary, run wide as you approach the barrier so you'll have an unobstructed view.

(2) If you are solidly superior to your opponents, take the lead immediately to assure an unobstructed view.

(3) Try this element of surprise: Accelerate into the water jump with approximately 500-600 yards remaining, then continue this acceleration to the finish!

Simulated Progressive Drills for Steeplechase

Testing #1

440—goal pace for steeplechase—hurdles and water jump
5½ laps—80-second 440 pace (No hurdles or water jump)
440—goal pace for steeplechase—hurdles and water jump

Testing #2

660—goal pace for steeplechase—hurdles and water jump
4½ laps—80-second 440 pace (No hurdles or water jump)
660—goal pace for steeplechase—hurdles and water jump

EVENT: Steeplechase: 21-day pattern

WEEK:

DATES:

DAY	WORKOUT	COMMENTS
M **1**	AM—30-minute run PM—(1) Hurdle technique instruction (2) 40-minute varied Fartlek run (3) 6 x 220 (30/30) (30 second 220/30 second rest)	Step #1 & #2 of hurdle progression.
Tu **2**	AM—30-minute run PM—10-mile run at a hard pace	On this run I time the runners, giving them their mile splits. Pace should be even and at a tempo difficult to maintain. Hurt a little on this run!
W **3**	AM—30-minute easy run PM—(1) Hurdle technique instruction (2) 30-minute easy run	Steps #1, 2, 3 of hurdle progression.

Th **4**	AM—30-minute run (1) 5 x 330 (110 rest) (goal pace for mile) (2) 30-minute easy run	
F **5**	AM—30-minute run PM—(1) Water jump technique instruction (2) Light grass run	Step #1 water jump progression.
Sa **6**	AM—Light run PM—(1) 1 x mile (date pace on chart) (2) 7 to 10 miles at sustained pace (3) 5 x 330—start at date pace and cut time down to below goal pace on last one (110 rest)	
Su **7**	12 miles at comfortable pace	

EVENT:

WEEK:

DATES:

DAY	WORKOUT	COMMENTS

M
 8
	AM—30-minute run
	
	 PM—(1) Hurdle drill
	     (2) 40-minute varied Fartlek run
	     (3) 8 x 220 (30/30)
		Hurdle drill step #4.

Tu **9**	AM—30-minute run PM—(1) 3-5 x mile (date pace) (880 rest) (2) Light run	
W **10**	AM—30-minute run PM—(1) Hurdle drill #5 (2) 30-minute run	

Th **11**	AM—30-minute run PM—(1) 5 x 440 (330 rest) (goal pace for mile) (2) Light grass run	
F **12**	AM—Light run PM—(1) Water progression drills #2, 3 (2) Light run	
Sa **13**	10:00 AM 12-mile control run PM—Light run	On this control run we start at a comfortable pace and each 2 miles cut the time down until last 2 miles are at date pace for mile.
Su **14**	12 to 15 miles at comfortable pace	

EVENT:

WEEK:

DATES:

DAY	WORKOUT	COMMENTS
M **15**	AM—30-minute run PM—(1) Hurdle drill step #6 (2) 30-minute varied Fartlek run (3) 10 x 220 (30/30)	
Tu **16**	AM—30-minute run PM—10 miles even pace (hard pace)	This is a control run with each mile split given.
W **17**	AM—30-minute run PM—(1) Water jump progression step #4 (2) Light grass	

Th 18	AM—30-minute run PM—4-mile effort on track at ½ effort. Four 36″ hurdles are placed at SC barrier marks	This drill is used to callous our runners for a Thursday preliminary followed by a Saturday final.
F 19	AM—Light run PM—Light run	

Sa 20	10:00 AM
	(1) 2 LAPS goal pace for steeple over 36″ hurdles (no water jump)
	  4 LAPS at 80-90 pace per 440
	  2 LAPS over hurdles at goal pace
	(2) 30 to 40 minutes
		This is a continuous run covering two miles, simulating competitive effort.

Su 21	12 to 15 miles comfortable pace	

EVENT: Steeplechase: 14-day pattern

WEEK:

DATES:

DAY	WORKOUT	COMMENTS
M **1**	AM—5 to 7 miles PM—(1) 45-minute varied Fartlek run (2) 6 x 220 (28/32)	

Tu
2
	AM—5 to 7 miles
	
	PM—(1) 2 x ¾ mile (goal pace for 5,000 meters) (660 rest)
	  (2) 2 x 880 (goal pace for 3,000 meters) (440 rest)
	  (3) 2 x 440 (goal pace for 1,500) (330 rest)
	  (4) Light grass run	

W **3**	AM—5 to 7 miles PM—(1) 4 x 220 over intermediate hurdles—placed SC barrier marks. (2) 7-mile steady run	

Th **4**	AM—5 to 7 miles PM—(1) 3 x 440 (goal pace for mile) (220 rest) (2) 30-minute light run	
F **5**	AM—5 miles easy PM—5 miles easy	
Sa **6**	COMPETITION Running a flat race, either over distance or under distance—normally a 1,500 or a 5,000 meter	
Su **7**	8 to 12 miles at comfortable pace	

EVENT:

WEEK:

DATES:

DAY	WORKOUT	COMMENTS
M **8**	AM—5 to 7 miles PM—45-minute varied Fartlek	

Tu
9
	AM—5 to 7 miles
	PM—(1) 440—660—440—220 (goal pace for mile)
	          (220—330 rest)
	      (2) 30-minute steady run	

W **10**	AM—5 to 7 miles PM—(1) 4 x water jump using plywood cover (2) 7 miles at steady pace	

Th **11**	AM—5 to 7 miles
	PM—(1) miles (80 pace) 4 intermediate hurdle per lap
	        at SC barrier marks
	    (2) Light grass	

F **12**	AM—Light grass PM—Light grass	
Sa **13**	COMPETITION Over 3,000-meter steeplechase	
Su **14**	8 to 12 easy miles	

EVENT: Steeplechase: 10-day pattern

WEEK:

DATES:

DAY	WORKOUT	COMMENTS
Th **1**	AM—5 to 7 miles PM—(1) 3 x 440 (55-57) (330 rest) (2) 20-minute grass run (3) 3 x 330—49-46-43 (110 rest)	
F **2**	AM—Light grass (20 minutes) PM—Light grass (30 minutes)	
Sa **3**	AM—Light grass PM—(1) 2 x mile—1st lap goal pace for SC, each lap faster ending with last lap goal for mile. Example: 67-65-63-58=4:13-4:15 (¾ mile rest) (2) 20 minutes grass	

Su 4	AM—Light run PM—Light run	
M 5	AM—5 to 7 miles PM—40-minute varied Fartlek run	
Tu 6	AM—5 to 7 miles PM—(1) 440-660-440-220 (goal pace for mile) (2) 20-minute grass run (3) 3 x 330—50-47-43 (110 rest)	
W 7	AM—20 to 30 minutes light grass PM—20 to 30 minutes light grass	

EVENT:

WEEK:

DATES:

DAY	WORKOUT	COMMENTS
Th **8**	AM—Light grass (20 minutes) PM—Trials for SC if necessary IF NOT (1) 8 x 220 (30) (2) Light grass	
F **9**	AM—Light grass (20 minutes) PM—Light grass (20 minutes)	
Sa **10**	CHAMPIONSHIP COMPETITION 3,000 meter steeplechase	

Testing #3

    440—goal pace for steeplechase—barriers and water jump
    880—80-second pace (flat)
    660—goal pace for steeplechase
    880—80-second pace
    440—goal pace for steeplechase

Testing #4

    880—goal pace for steeplechase—barriers and water jump
    3½ laps—80-second pace
    880—goal pace for steeplechase—barriers and water jump

Testing #5

    880—80-second pace
    Mile—goal pace for steeplechase—using barriers and water jump
    880—80-second pace

Testing #6

    3 laps—goal pace for steeplechase—barriers and water jump
    2 laps—80 pace (flat)
    3 laps—goal pace for steeplechase—barriers and water jump

Testing #7

    2 laps—goal pace for steeplechase—barriers and water jump
    1 lap—80 pace
    2 laps—goal pace for steeplechase—barriers and water jump
    1 lap—80 pace
    2 laps—goal pace for steeplechase—barriers and water jump

5,000 AND 10,000 METERS

The five and ten kilometers are considered to be the true distance events of track. Occasionally a world class miler will

Craig Virgin,
one of the top U.S. runners
in the 5,000 and the 10,000.

compete at 5,000 meters. It is rare to find a miler moving all the
way to the 10,000 meters.

Most runners will compete at the shorter distances as long as
they can be successful. As a runner matures and loses his leg
speed, he will move up to the longer events.

The United States has had limited success in these distance
events. This is primarily because we do not provide a program
for our postgraduate students that would give them a chance to
mature and "move up" into these events.

I believe it is a mistake to rush young runners into these events, which require development of sub-cellular components within skeletal muscles that are responsible for prolonged endurance aerobic metabolism.

At Oregon we attempt to rotate our runners so they will not be competing over the 5,000-meter distance every week. Our runners will run a maximum of three 10,000-meter races during the track season. Most of our distance men will also have the opportunity to compete in the 1,500 and the 3,000-meter steeplechase. Our running patterns are designed to give them this range.

The patterns presented are broken down into 21-day noncompetitive training, 14-day competitive, and 10-day championship preparations.

Tactics for 5,000 and 10,000

The five and ten kilometers are long enough for varying tactics. Tactics or strategies employed can depend upon many factors. Strengths and weaknesses of opponent, weather conditions, and your own strengths and weaknesses are among the key factors.

A tactic is not an advantage unless you have calloused yourself to this particular move and your opponent has not. Then, of course, you must get him to fall for the tactic.

The easiest way to run a 13:24, 5,000 meters is to run 65 seconds per 440. That is, run even pace. If you are throwing in several surges but averaging 65 per lap and your opponent is running even pace and averaging 65 per lap, he has the advantage! He is expending less energy.

The longer the race the more time there is to think. Obviously this becomes a factor in race strategies. Running in a pack usually results in enough jostling to keep the runner's mind active. Suddenly the race is nearing the end. The runner has not had time to think about physical fatigue. He can gain the advantage if he can break this mental and physical contact by use of tactics.

A survey of tactics follows. Remember, the element of surprise

EVENT: 5,000-10,000: 21-day pattern

WEEK:

DATES:

DAY	WORKOUT	COMMENTS

M **1**	AM—5 to 8 miles
	
	PM—(1) 60-minute varied Fartlek run
	    (2) 6 x 220 (30/30) (30-second 220)
	                (30-second rest)	

Tu **2**	AM—5 to 8 miles PM—12-mile run control pace 5:20-5:30 per mile	
W **3**	AM—5 to 8 miles PM—40-minute easy run	

Th **4**	AM—5 to 8 miles PM—(1) 440—660—440—220 (goal pace for mile) (2) 30-minute run (3) 6 x 330 cut-down (110 rest)	
F **5**	AM—Light run PM—Light run	
Sa **6**	AM—Light run PM—10-mile run at 5:00 pace	
Su **7**	15 miles comfortable pace	

EVENT:

WEEK:

DATES:

DAY	WORKOUT	COMMENTS
M **8**	AM—5 to 8 miles PM—(1) 45-minute varied Fartlek run (2) 8 x 220 (30/30)	
Tu **9**	AM—5 to 8 miles PM—10 miles at 5:20 pace	
W **10**	AM—5 to 8 miles PM—Light run	

Th **11**	AM—5 to 8 miles PM—(1) 1 mile (date pace) (2) 4 miles at 80 pace	
F **12**	AM—Light run PM—Light run	
Sa **13**	AM—Light run PM—(1) 6 x 880 (goal pace 5,000) (440 rest) (2) 5-mile run	
Su **14**	15 miles comfortable pace	

EVENT:

WEEK:

DATES:

DAY	WORKOUT	COMMENTS
M **15**	AM—5 to 8 miles PM—(1) 45-minute varied Fartlek run (2) 10 x 220 (30/30)	
Tu **16**	AM—5 to 8 miles PM—12-mile run control pace 5:20-5:30 per mile	
W **17**	AM—4 to 8 miles PM—5 to 8 miles	

Th **18**	AM—4 to 8 miles PM—(1) 2 to 3 miles (40/30 drill) (2) Light grass	On this drill we run a 40-second 220 followed by a 30-second 220—70 for the 440. When runners can no longer carry pace, they stop.
F **19**	AM—Light run PM—Light run	
Sa **20**	AM—Light run PM—(1) Simulated 10,000-meter drill (2) Light run	
Su **21**	12 to 15 miles comfortable pace	

EVENT: 5,000-10,000: 14-day pattern

WEEK:

DATES:

DAY	WORKOUT	COMMENTS
M **1**	AM—5 to 7 miles PM—(1) 40-minute varied Fartlek run (2) 6 x 220 (30/30)	
Tu **2**	AM—5 to 7 miles PM—(1) 6 x 880 (date pace for 5,000) (440 rest) (2) 20-minute grass run (3) 4 x 330 cut-down	
W **3**	AM—5 to 7 miles PM—40-minute steady run	

Th 4	AM—5 to 7 miles PM—(1) 6 x 330 (45) (or goal pace for mile) (2) 30-minute grass run	
F 5	AM—5 miles PM—20 to 30 minutes light grass run	
Sa 6	AM—Light grass run PM—COMPETITION 5,000 or 1,500 (reverse following week)	
Su 7	12 miles comfortable pace	

EVENT:

WEEK:

DATES:

DAY	WORKOUT	COMMENTS
M **8**	AM—5 to 8 miles PM—(1) 60-minute varied Fartlek run (2) 6 x 220 (30/30)	
Tu **9**	AM—5 to 8 miles PM—(1) 440—660—440—220 (goal pace for mile) (2) 2-4 x 660—440—330—220—110 (date pace for 5,000)	
W **10**	AM—5 to 8 miles PM—5 to 8 miles	

Th **11**	AM—5 to 8 miles PM—(1) 4 miles on track (in flats) at 75-80 pace (2) Light grass run-out	
F **12**	AM—5-mile run PM—20 to 30 minutes grass run	
Sa **13**	AM—Light run PM—COMPETITION either 1,500 or 5,000 or 10,000	
Su **14**	12 miles easy	

EVENT: 5,000-10,000: 10-day championship pattern

WEEK:

DATES:

DAY	WORKOUT	COMMENTS
Th **1**	AM—5 to 8 miles PM—(1) 4 x ¾ mile (goal pace for 5,000) (880 rest) (2) 3 x mile cut-down (example: 5:00—4:40—4:26) (3) Light grass run	
F **2**	AM—Light run PM—Light run	
Sa **3**	AM—Light run PM—(1) Mile (date pace) (2) 2 x 660—440—330—220—110 (date pace for 5,000) (3) Light grass run	

Su **4**	12 to 15 miles comfortable pace	
M **5**	AM—5 to 8 miles 11 AM (1) 2 x 220 (26) (2) grass run—1 mile PM—5 miles easy	
Tu **6**	AM—5 to 8 miles PM—(1) 4 miles at 75-80 pace (2) 3 x 330—50-47-44 (110 rest)	
W **7**	AM—2 to 4 miles easy PM—30-minute easy grass run	

EVENT:

WEEK:

DATES:

DAY	WORKOUT	COMMENTS
Th **8**	AM—Light grass PM—Qualifying competition	
F **9**	20-minute light grass run	
Sa **10**	AM—Light grass run PM—Finals of Competition	

Oregon's crop of young
5,000- and 10,000-meter runners.

is the best tactic; use your own imagination. There are as many different tactics as there are runners!

(1) Throw in a strong surge in the middle of the 5,000 or 10,000 to attempt to break contact with your opponents. Once contact is broken, you can settle down to a steady pace. In most cases, the opponent, once broken, will remain the same distance back. If he does surge with you and has not calloused himself to this maneuver, he jeopardizes his finish.

(2) If you are racing an opponent with greater speed, make your move for the finish anywhere from three laps to a 660 from the finish. Murray Halberg won the 1960 Olympic 5,000 by throwing in a 58-second 400 with three laps remaining. He gained 40 yards on this surprise move.

Although his opponents gained on him over the remaining two laps, he still won by seven yards!

(3) Make a strong surge (pick up the pace) in running against the wind and relax down the back stretch with the wind to your back.

(4) Learn to sprint-float-sprint over the final 165 to the finish.

(5) Let your opponent get approximately 15 yards on you and wait for the final 330 for your own surge. He may think he has broken contact and get careless.

(6) When you have the lead and are in your final sprint for the finish, go at what is about 95 percent effort and be ready to accept one more challenge! Be relaxed and ready for another five percent!

Simulated Progressive Drills for 5,000 Meters

Drill #1

440—goal pace
880—80-90 pace
440—goal pace
880—80-90 pace
440—goal pace
880—80-90 pace
440—goal pace
880—80-90 pace

Drill #2

880—goal pace
3 laps—90-90 pace
880—goal pace
3 laps—80-90 pace
880—goal pace

Drill #3

2½ laps—goal pace
2 laps—80-90 pace

2½ laps—goal pace
2 laps—80-90 pace
3 laps—goal pace

Drill #4

3 laps—goal pace
3 laps—80-90 pace
3 laps—goal pace
3 laps—80-90 pace
(Can reverse this drill)

Drill #5

3 laps—goal pace
2 laps—80-90 pace
2 laps—goal pace
2 laps—80-90 pace
3 laps—goal pace

Drill #6

3 laps—goal pace
1½ laps—80-90 pace
3 laps—goal pace
1½ laps—80-90 pace
3 laps—goal pace

Simulated Progressive Drills for 10,000 Meters

Drill #1

440—goal pace
440—80-90 pace
Continue for a total of 24 laps.

Drill #2

880—goal pace
440—80-90 pace
Continue for a total of 24 laps.

Drill #*3*

   3 laps—goal pace
   2 laps—80-90 pace
Continue for a total of 25 laps.

Drill #*4*

   4 laps—goal pace
   2 laps—80-90 pace
Continue for a total of 24 laps.

Drill #*5*

   4 laps—goal pace
   660—90 pace (440)
   4 laps—goal pace
   660—90 pace (440)
   4 laps—goal pace
   660—90 pace (440)
   4 laps—goal pace
   660—90 pace (440)
   4 laps—goal pace

Drill #*6*

   4 laps—goal pace
   1 lap—80-90
   4 laps—goal pace
   1 lap—80-90
   4 laps—goal pace
   1 lap—80-90
   4 laps—goal pace
   1 lap—80-90
   4 laps—goal pace

chapter five

the program of steve prefontaine, competitor

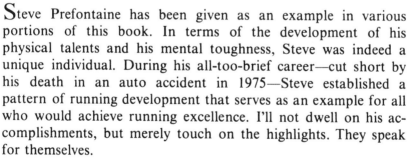

Steve Prefontaine has been given as an example in various portions of this book. In terms of the development of his physical talents and his mental toughness, Steve was indeed a unique individual. During his all-too-brief career—cut short by his death in an auto accident in 1975—Steve established a pattern of running development that serves as an example for all who would achieve running excellence. I'll not dwell on his accomplishments, but merely touch on the highlights. They speak for themselves.

1969 (his final year of high school) - Set national prep two-mile record (8:41.5); placed second behind Gerry Lindgren in two-mile race at Hawaii while running for United States national team (8:46.0); placed second in 5,000 meters during U.S.-West Germany meet in Augsburg (14:07.0).

1969 (as Oregon freshman) - third in NCAA cross-country championships, behind winner, Lindgren, and runner-up, Mike Ryan.

5/16/70 - Won Pac-8 three-mile title (13:27.8).

6/5/70 - Set Oregon freshman record in mile (3:57.4).

6/20/70 - Won NCAA three-mile race in meet record time (13:22.0).

7/26/70 - Won 1,500-meter run at Moscow Invitational in Russia (3:44.0).

11/23/70 - Won NCAA cross-country crown in meet record time (28:00.2).

5/22/71 - Won Pac-8 Championship mile (4:01.5) and three-mile (13:18.0).

6/19/71 - Won NCAA three-mile second time in record time (13:20.2).

6/25/71 - Won AAU three-mile title in meet record time (12:58.6).

7/3/71 - Won 5,000-meter race in U.S.-Russia meet in American and Collegiate record time (13:30.4).

8/3/71 - Won 5,000-meter run in Pan-Am Games (13:52.5).

1/29/72 - Established American Collegiate indoor record for two-mile (8:26.6).

4/23/72 - Ran his fastest mile (3:56.7).

4/29/72 - Established American and Collegiate 5,000-meter record (13:29.8).

5/20/72 - Won third straight Pac-8 Championship three-mile (13:32.2).

6/3/72 - Won third straight NCAA three-mile title (13:31.4) to become third American to win three NCAA distance championships.

7/9/72 - Won 5,000-meter championship in Olympic Trials in American record time (13:22.8).

9/10/72 - Took fourth in finals of Olympic games in 5,000 meters (13:28.4).

3/24/73 - Established American and Collegiate records for six-mile run at Bakersfield Invitational (27:09.4).

4/14/73 - Ran fastest double ever for mile (3:56.8) and three-mile (13:06.4).

5/19/73 - Won his fourth straight Pac-8 meet title at three miles with meet record (13:10.4).

6/9/73 - Won his fourth straight NCAA title in three miles with meet record (13:05.3).

11/19/73 - Won his third straight NCAA cross-country title (28:14.8).

The running patterns presented in chapter four cover a specific period of time and are designed for general use, with room for adaptation. In this chapter I would like to show how these patterns were applied to one individual—Steve Prefontaine. This is not a diary of his workouts, but an outline I asked him to follow. "Pre" believed in the program, and, with few exceptions, did what was asked of him.

ONE-YEAR PROGRAM OF STEVE PREFONTAINE

The following program is for the summer of 1972. It covers a 57-day period of preparation for the Munich Olympics and "Pre's" competition.

I might point out that "Pre" finished fourth in this competition. The finals were delayed a day because of the Israeli tragedy. I believe the agitation of the delay and his frustrations over the incident combined with his inexperience cost him a higher placing.

EVENT: Steve Prefontaine

WEEK:

DATES: September-June

DAY	September WORKOUT	COMMENTS
M	AM—3 to 5 miles PM—Light grass run	
Tu	AM—Light grass run PM—(1) 8 x 880 (cut-downs) 　　(2) 6 miles (Homer-varied) 　　(3) 12 x 330—4—50-52 　　　　　　　4—48-50 　　　　　　　4—cut-down	
W	AM—5-mile run PM—5-mile run (light on hills)	

Th	AM—3-mile run PM—9 x 330 (easy—medium—hard) Intervals	
F	AM—Light grass run PM—Light grass run	
Sa	10 AM (1) 10-mile run (3 x ¾ 3:15—3:12—3:16) (2) 6 x 330 cut-downs on track PM—2 miles light grass run 　　　8 to 12 grass 110's	
Su	Light grass	

EVENT:

WEEK: #2

DATES: October

DAY	WORKOUT	COMMENTS
M	AM—3 to 5 miles PM—3 to 6 miles	
Tu	AM—3 to 5 miles light PM—(1) 3 x ¾ cut-downs (track) 　　(2) 3 x 1 mile 　　(3) 12 x 330 (easy—medium—hard)	
W	AM—3 to 6 miles PM—5 to 10 miles	

Th	AM—3 to 5 miles—12 x 110 (easy—medium—medium hard) PM—(1) 24 x 165 (24-26) (55-yard rest) (2) 3 to 5 miles Fartlek (3) 6 x 330 cut-downs	
F	AM—3 miles light PM—3 to 5 miles light Film 4:10 PM	
Sa	10 AM 3-mile trial run PM—12 x 330 (easy—medium—hard)	
Su	12 to 16 miles	

EVENT:

WEEK: #3

DATES: October

DAY	WORKOUT	COMMENTS

M	AM—3-mile run
	
	PM—Light grass
	        3 laps—12 x 110 (easy—medium—medium)
	        3 laps—12 x 110 (easy—medium—hard)
	        3 laps—12 x 110 (easy—medium—medium)	

Tu	AM—3 to 5 miles light
	
	PM—(1) 6 x 330—(45-47)
	     (2) 10 miles (1 hour—1:10)
	     (3) 6 x 330 cut-downs	

W	AM—3 to 5 miles
	
	PM—(1) 6 to 10 miles
	     (2) 6 to 9 miles grass (110 x 3) (easy—medium—
	           medium hard)	

Th	AM—3 to 4 miles
	
	PM—(1) 6 x 220—35 (220 rest)
	        6 x 220—33
	        6 x 220—31
	(2) 3 miles light
	(3) 6 x 330 cut-downs	

F	AM—Light run PM—Light run	
Sa	10 AM 10 miles steady	
Su	12 to 15 miles	

WEEK: #4

DATES: October

DAY	WORKOUT	COMMENTS
M	AM—3 to 5 miles PM—4 to 7 miles	
Tu	AM—3 miles—6 x 110 (easy—medium) PM—(1) Mile (64-66 pace) 　　　(2) 12 x 330 　　　(3) 6 x 330 cut-downs	
W	AM—3 to 5 miles PM—10 miles steady (film first)	

Th	AM—3 to 5 miles PM—(1) 12 x 165 (24-26) (55-yard rest) (2) 3 to 5 miles (3) 6 x 330 cut-downs	
F	AM—3 to 5 miles light PM—3 to 5 miles light	
Sa	10 AM (1) 4 x ¾ (67 pace up or down 1) (2) 3 x 1 mile—73's 70's 68's PM—Light jog 2 to 3 miles grass	
Su	Light jog	

EVENT:

WEEK: #5

DATES: October

DAY	WORKOUT	COMMENTS
M	AM—3 to 5 miles PM—3 to 5 miles	
Tu	AM—Light run PM—(1) Easy warm-up (2) 4 x 330—48-50; 4 x 330—44-46; 4 x 330—48-50 (all with 110 rest) (3) 3 miles light (4) 6 x 220—2 in 32-34; 2 in 30-32; 2 in 28-30	
W	AM—Light run—3 to 5 miles PM—3 to 6 miles	

Th	AM—3 to 5 miles PM—(1) 1 to 2 miles warm-up—4 to 6 easy strides (2) 12 x 165—24-26 (55-yard rest) (3) 3 miles light (4) 8 x 220 (32-34)	
F	AM—Light run PM—Light run	
Sa	Northern Division Cross-Country Championships	
Su	12 to 15 miles easy	

EVENT:

WEEK: #6

DATES: November

DAY	WORKOUT	COMMENTS
M	AM—3 to 5 miles light PM—3 to 6 miles light	
Tu	AM—3 to 5 miles PM—(1) 10 miles (3 x ¾ timed at beginning, middle, and end of run) (2) 9 x 330—3 in 50 3 in 48 3 cut-downs	
W	AM—3 to 5 miles PM—(1) 6-mile run (2) 9 x 110 (easy—medium—medium hard)	

Th	AM—(1) Mile jog (2) 12 x 330 (4 in 52; 4 in 50; 4 in 48; with 110 rest) PM—(1) Warm-up (2) 2 x 220—27 (+-1) (3) 6-mile run (4) 6 x 220—34 (+-1)	
F	AM—Light run PM—Light run	
Sa	10 AM (1) 3 x 1 mile—67 (+-1) (880 rest) (2) 12 x 330 PM—3 to 6 miles light	
Su	12 to 15 miles easy	

EVENT:

WEEK: #7

DATES: November

DAY	WORKOUT	COMMENTS
M	AM—3 to 5 miles light PM—3 to 6 miles light	
Tu	AM—3 miles—9 x 110 (easy—medium—medium hard) PM—(1) 6 x 330 (52-54) 6 x 330 (50-52) 6 x 330 (48-50) (2) Light grass (3) 4 x 110 (medium)	
W	AM—3 to 5 miles PM—3 to 6 miles	

Th	AM—3 to 5 miles PM—(1) Warm-up (2) 2 x 165 (⅞ effort) (3) 5 miles light (4) 6 x 220 (32-35)	
F	7 AM—3 miles light PM—Jog cross-country course	
Sa	10 AM Pac-8 Cross-Country Meet	
Su	10 to 15 miles (7-minute mile pace)	

EVENT:

WEEK: #8

DATES: November

DAY	WORKOUT	COMMENTS
M	AM—3 to 5 miles light PM—3 to 5 miles light	
Tu	AM—Light run PM—(1) 12 x 440 (70 seconds) (110 rest) (2) 2 x ¾ (70—68) (3) 4 x 330 (50—48—46—44) (4) Light grass	
W	AM—3 miles PM—10 miles at 7-minute mile pace	

Th	AM—Light run PM—Light run	
F	AM—Light run PM—(1) 4 miles at 80 pace (2) 6 x 330 (48-50)	
Sa	Travel—Light run	
Su	Light run	

EVENT:

WEEK: #9

DATES: November

DAY	WORKOUT	COMMENTS
M	NCAA Championships	
Tu	AM—Light run (travel) PM—Light run (travel)	
W	AM—Light grass runs PM—Light grass runs	

Th	AM—Light grass runs PM—Light grass runs	
F	AM—Light grass runs PM—Light grass runs	
Sa	PM—10 miles at 6:30 pace	
Su	Light grass run	

WEEK: #10

DATES: December

DAY	WORKOUT	COMMENTS
M	AM—Light run PM—Light run	
Tu	AM—3 to 5 miles PM—(1) 12 x 440 (65) (60-second rest) (2) 4 x ¾ (70) (440 rest) (3) 6 x 330 cut-down	
W	AM—Light run PM—Light run	

Th	(1) 6 x 330 (44) (2) 10 miles at 7-minute pace (3) 6 x 330 cut-down	
F	AM—Light run PM—Light run	
Sa	10:30 AM (1) Mile 64 (+-1) (2) 4 x 660 (70)—440 (68)—330 (49)—220 (32)—110 (15) sets	
Su	15-mile run	

EVENT:

WEEK: #11

DATES: December

DAY	WORKOUT	COMMENTS
M	AM—3 to 5 miles PM—4 to 7 miles Fartlek	
Tu	AM—3 to 4 miles PM—(1) 2 x ¾ mile goal pace (3-4 minute rest) 2 x 880 goal pace (2-3 minute rest) 2 x 440—62 (+-1) (60-90 second rest) (2) 2 to 4 x 330—52; 2 to 4 x 330—50; 2 to 4 x 330 cut-down	
W	AM—3 to 5 miles PM—6 to 10 miles steady Fartlek	

Th	AM—3 to 5 miles
	
	PM—(1) 16-24 x 220—32 pace (28-second rest)
	     (2) Light Fartlek
	     (3) 2 x 165 (20-22)	

F	AM—3 to 4 miles PM—3 to 5 miles	

Sa	10:30 AM—(1) ¾ effort (date pace) 3 miles
	     (2) 6 miles
	     (3) 6 x 330 cut-downs	

Su	long—easy 8—10—12—15	

EVENT:

WEEK: #12

DATES: December

DAY	WORKOUT	COMMENTS
M	AM—5 to 7 miles PM—40-minute varied Fartlek run	
Tu	AM—5 to 7 miles PM—(1) 220—440—660—220—440—220 (62 pace) (2) 7 miles (3) 3 x 330 (51—47—43)	
W	AM—7-mile run PM—7 to 10 miles steady pace	

Th	AM—40-minute run
	
	PM—(1) 9 x 330—3 easy pace
	                      3 medium pace
	                      3 hard pace
	     (2) 7 miles	

F	AM—5-mile run PM—7-mile run	
Sa	10:00 AM (1) 1 x 880—(2:04) (2) 30th Ave. (6-minute pace)—9-miles (3) 4 x 330 (52—49—46—43)	
Su	12 to 15 miles easy	

157

WEEK: #13

DATES: December

DAY	WORKOUT	COMMENTS
M	AM—40-minute run PM—40-minute varied Fartlek run	
Tu	AM—30-minute run PM—(1) 6 x 880 (2) 5-mile run (3) 6 x 330 cut-down	
W	AM—5 to 7 miles PM—7 to 10 miles steady comfortable pace	

Th	AM—30-minute run PM—(1) 11 x 165 (23) (55-yard rest) (2) 5-mile run (3) 3 x 330 (52—48—44)	165's are to simulate distance for indoor racing.
F	AM—Light grass run PM—Light grass run	
Sa	10 AM (1) Mile at date pace (66's) (2) 6-minute pace (9 miles) (3) 6 x 330 cut-down	
Su	12 to 15 miles easy	

EVENT:

WEEK: #14

DATES: December/January

DAY	WORKOUT	COMMENTS
M	AM—5 to 8 miles PM—45-minute varied Fartlek run	
Tu	AM—30-minute light run PM—(1) 4 x 660 (66)—440 (63)—330 (47)—220 (31)— 110 (14) (2) 4-mile run	
W	AM—7-mile run PM—7 miles steady pace	

Th	AM—5-mile run PM—(1) 11 x 165 (23) (110 rest) (2) 30-minute run (3) 3 x 330 (49—46—43)	
F	AM—Light run PM—Light run	
Sa	10 AM (1) 4 x 880 (62's) (660 rest) (2) 2 x 660 (70)—440 (66)—330 (48)—220 (30)—110 (14) PM—Light grass run	
Su	12 to 15 miles	

WEEK: #15

DATES: January

DAY	WORKOUT	COMMENTS
M	AM—Light run PM—40-minute varied Fartlek run	
Tu	AM—5-mile run PM—(1) 4 x 220 (31) (220 rest) 1 x ¾ (70) (440 rest) 4 x 220 (31) 1 x ¾ (68) 4 x 220 (31)	
W	AM—Light run PM—Light run	

Th	AM—7 miles PM—(1) 12-20 x 220 (31) (2) 20-minute run	
F	AM—Light run PM—Light run	

Sa	10 AM
	(1) 1 x mile (4:09—4:12)
	    2 x 880 (2:03—2:06)
	    1 x 440 (60)
	    2 x 220 (28)
	(2) 20-minute run	

Su	12 to 15 miles	

EVENT:

WEEK: #16

DATES: January

DAY	WORKOUT	COMMENTS
M	AM—4 to 7 miles PM—45-minute varied Fartlek run	
Tu	AM—30-minute run PM—(1) 1 x 440 (660—440—220) (goal pace for mile) (2) 30-minute run (3) 4 x 330 cut-down (track)	
W	AM—30-minute easy run PM—30-minute easy run	

Th	AM—5-mile run PM—(1) 11 x 165 (22.5) (55-yard rest) (2) 20-minute run (3) 3 x 330 (51—47—44) (110 rest)	
F	AM—5 to 8 miles PM—Travel to Los Angeles Light grass run	
Sa	AM—30-minute light run PM—Sunkist Invitational 2-Mile	
Su	Travel—light run	

WEEK: #17

DATES: January

DAY	WORKOUT	COMMENTS
M	AM—4 to 7 miles PM—40-minute varied Fartlek run	
Tu	AM—4 to 7 miles PM—(1) 440—660—440—220 (all at 60-62) (2) 2 miles at 80 (3) 5 x 330 (47)	
W	AM—4 to 7 miles PM—40-minute run	

Th	AM—4 to 7 miles PM—(1) 5 x 330 (47) 　　　(2) Easy run 　　　(3) 5 x 110 (17-16-15-14-13)	
F	AM—Light runs PM—Light runs	
Sa	AM—Light runs PM—Portland Indoor (63's first mile)	
Su	Long easy run	

EVENT:

WEEK: #18

DATES: January/February

DAY	WORKOUT	COMMENTS
M	AM—3 miles—12 x 110 (easy—medium—medium hard) PM—40-minute run at comfortable pace	
Tu	AM—3 to 5 miles PM—(1) 440—660—440—220 (with Roscoe) 　　(2) 2 to 4 set 660—Breakdown on sawdust	
W	AM—5 mile run PM—6 to 10-mile Fartlek	

Th	AM—3 miles—4 x 110 (16-15-14-13) PM—(1) 2 x 220 (25-26) (2) 6 x 165 (Middle pick-up) (3) Light Fartlek	
F	AM—Light run PM—Light run	
Sa	(1) 3 x 330 (45-46) (2) 1 x 880 (1:56—1:58) (3) 2 x 440 (60) (+-1) (4) 4 x 220 (29-30) (5) 2 sets 660 down (72-67-48-30)	
Su	AM—Long easy run—6 to 12 miles PM—Light Homer Fartlek	

WEEK: #19

DATES: February

DAY	WORKOUT	COMMENTS
M	AM—(1) 3 to 5 miles (2) 4 x 110 (17-16-15-14) PM—(1) 40-minute Homer Fartlek	
Tu	AM—3 miles light PM—(1) 6 x 330—First 220—31 110—14 (2) 6 x 165 (21) (3) Light Fartlek run (4) 4 x 110 grass	
W	AM—(1) 3-mile run (2) 4 x 110 (17—16—15—14) PM—40-minute Fartlek run	

Th	AM—3 to 5 miles PM—(1) 2 x 220 (27-28) (2) Light Fartlek run	
F	PM—COMPETITION Los Angeles Mile	
Sa	12 to 15 miles Fartlek run	
Su	AM—Light run PM—2 miles grass 8 x 110 at medium pace	

EVENT:

WEEK: #20

DATES: February

DAY	WORKOUT	COMMENTS
M	AM—(1) 4-mile run 　　　(2) 4 x 110 (18-17-16-15) PM—(1) 40-minute Homer Fartlek 　　　(2) 4 x 110 (17-16-15-14)	
Tu	AM—3 to 5 miles PM—(1) 2 x ¾ (66's) 　　　　　2 x 880 (64) 　　　　　2 x 440 (62) 　　　(2) 2 miles grass or sawdust 　　　(3) 8 x 330 (48)	
W	AM—(1) 4-mile run 　　　(2) 4 x 110 (17-16-15-14) PM—(1) 45-minute Lydian Fartlek 　　　(2) 4 x 110 grass	

Th	AM—3 to 5 miles PM—(1) During warm-up 6 x log for steeple (2) 2 x 165—sprint 55—float 55—sprint 55 (3) 2 x 220 (34) over hurdles (4) 12 x 220 (32) (110 rest) (5) Light Fartlek	
F	AM—(1) 3 to 4 miles (2) 4 x 110 grass PM—Light grass run	
Sa	10 AM (1) 6 miles at 75's (2) 3 miles grass (3) 6 x 330 cut-downs	
Su	15-mile run	

EVENT:

WEEK: #21

DATES: February

DAY	WORKOUT	COMMENTS
M	AM—3 to 5 miles PM—(1) 30 to 40-minute Homer Fartlek (2) 4 x 110 grass (17-16-15-14)	
Tu	AM—3 to 4 miles light PM—(1) 4 x 330—48; 4 x 330—46; 4 x 330—44 (all sawdust) (2) 2 to 3 x 660 (70)—440 (66)—330 (48)—220 (30)—110 (grass) (3) Light grass jog-out	
W	AM—3 to 5 miles PM—(1) 40-minute Lydian Fartlek (2) 4 x 110 (16-15-14-13)	

Th	AM—Light run PM—(1) 6 x 330 (42-44) (2) 30-minute light Fartlek	
F	AM—Light runs PM—Light runs	
Sa	10 AM (1) 4 x ¾ at 65's (2) 3 x 660 (70)—440 (66)—330 (48)—220 (30)—110 (grass)	
Su	12 to 15 miles comfortable pace	

EVENT:

WEEK: #22

DATES: March

DAY	WORKOUT	COMMENTS
M	AM—(1) 3 to 5 miles (2) 4 x 110 (17-16-15-14) PM—Light Fartlek run	
Tu	AM—Light run PM—16 to 20 x 440—64-66 (220 rest)	
W	AM—3 to 5 miles PM—40-minute steady Fartlek	

Th	AM—Light grass run
	
	PM—(1) 2 x 220 (26)
	    (2) 30-minute Homer Fartlek
	    (3) 2 sets—660 (70)—440 (67)—330 (47)—220
	         (30)—110 (grass)	

F	AM—Light run PM—Light run	

Sa	AM—(1) 6 x 330 (43-45)
	    (2) 9-mile steady Fartlek
	    (3) 6 x 330 cut-downs
	
	PM—3 to 4 miles light 4 x 110 (16-15-14-13)	

Su	8 to 12 miles	

EVENT:

WEEK: #23

DATES: March

DAY	WORKOUT	COMMENTS
M	AM—Light run PM—Light run	
Tu	AM—Light run PM—(1) Mile 61-62's (2) 2 to 4 x 660 sets (sawdust)	
W	AM—Light grass PM—Light grass	

Th	AM—Light run PM—(1) 2 x 165—sprint—float—sprint (2) Light Fartlek (3) 4 x 110 (17-16-15-14)	
F	Light run	
Sa	10 AM (1) 2 x ¾ at 65's (2) 12 x 440 at 64-66 (3) Light Fartlek PM—Light grass—4 x 110 (17-16-15-14)	
Su	12 to 15 miles light steady	

EVENT:

WEEK: #24

DATES: March

DAY	WORKOUT	COMMENTS
M	AM—Easy runs when convenient PM—Easy runs when convenient	See me for working around your final exam schedule!
Tu	AM—Easy run PM—(1) 6 x 880 (date pace for 5,000) 　　(2) 20-minute run 　　(3) 3 x 330 (48-45-42)	
W	AM—Easy runs when convenient PM—Easy runs when convenient	

Th	AM—Light run PM—(1) 6 x 330 (44) (110 rest) (2) 30-minute run	
F	AM—Easy runs when convenient PM—Easy runs when convenient	
Sa	AM—Light run PM—Oregon Invitational Relays	
Su	12 to 15 miles easy	

EVENT:

WEEK: #25

DATES: March

DAY	WORKOUT	COMMENTS
M	AM—Light run PM—Light run	
Tu	AM—Light run PM—(1) 440—660—440—220 at (60) 　　(2) 1 x ¾—880 (67)—660 (66)—440 (65)—330 　　　　　(64)—220 (47)—110 (30) 　　(3) Light grass	
W	AM—Light run PM—(1) 4 x 330 (50) 　　　　4 x 330 (48) 　　　　4 x 330 (46) 　　(2) Light grass	

Th 4	AM—Light run PM—Light grass	
F 5	AM—Light run PM—(1) Grass warm-up (2) 2 x 220 (28) (3) Light grass	
Sa 6	COMPETITION Washington (Mile)	
Su 7	12 to 16 miles	

EVENT:

WEEK: #26

DATES: April

DAY	WORKOUT	COMMENTS
M	AM—3 to 5 miles PM—40-minute varied Fartlek run	
Tu	AM—Light run PM—(1) 4 x 440 (66) (110 rest) 　　　 4 x 440 (64) (110 rest) 　　　 4 x 440 (62) (110 rest) 　　　 (440 rest between sets) 　(2) 2 to 3 sets of 660 breakdown on sawdust	
W	AM—Light run 11:30 AM—Mile grass—4 x 110 PM—30 to 40 minutes grass Fartlek	

Th	AM—Light run PM—(1) 12 x 165 (24) (110 rest) (2) 2 miles of grass or sawdust at comfortable pace (3) 4 x 110 (15-14-13-12)	
F	AM—Light run PM—Travel and light grass	
Sa	CALIFORNIA COMPETITION 3-mile	
Su	12 to 15 miles comfortable pace	

EVENT:

WEEK: #27

DATES: April

DAY	WORKOUT	COMMENTS
M	AM—3 to 5 miles 11 AM (1) Mile warm-up (2) 2 x 220 (27) accelerate off turn PM—45-minute varied Fartlek run	
Tu	AM—5-mile run PM—(1) 2½—1½ laps at goal for mile 　　　(2) 4-mile run at 80 pace	
W	AM—5 to 7 miles 11 AM Mile warm-up—4 x 110 (15-14-13-12) PM—Light grass run	

Th	AM—5-mile run PM—(1) 3 x 440 (59—57—55) (440 rest) (2) 4-mile run at 80 pace	
F	AM—Light grass run PM—Light grass run	
Sa	AM—Light grass run PM—UCLA COMPETITION (Mile)	
Su	12 to 15 miles easy	

EVENT:

WEEK: #28

DATES: April

DAY	WORKOUT	COMMENTS
M	40-minute varied Fartlek run	

Tu	AM—4 to 7 miles
	
	PM—(1) 4 x 880 (62-63) (440 rest)
	    (2) 20-minute run
	    (3) 6 x 330—2—48
	                2—46
	                2—44	

W	AM—40-minute run PM—40-minute run	

Th	AM—30-minute run PM—(1) 3 x 330 (48) 3 x 220 (31) 3 x 110 (13.5) (2) 20 to 30-minute light run	
F	AM—Light run PM—Light run	
Sa	Twilight—6-mile run	
Su	12 to 15 miles easy	

EVENT:

WEEK: #29

DATES: April/May

DAY	WORKOUT	COMMENTS
M	AM—5 to 7 miles PM—40-minute varied Fartlek run	

Tu	AM—5 to 8 miles
	
	PM—(1) 6 x 330 (47)
	     (2) 7 to 10 miles
	     (3) 6 x 330 cut-down	

W	AM—7 to 10 miles easy pace PM—7 to 10 miles easy pace	

Th	AM—4 to 7 miles PM—(1) 3 x 330 (46) 　　　　3 x 220 (29) 　　　　3 x 120 (13) 　　(2) 20-minute light run	
F	AM—4 to 7 miles PM—4 to 7 miles	
Sa	10AM 1 x ¾—72—70—68 (flats) 10-mile run 1 x ¾—70—68—66	
Su	Easy long run	

EVENT:

WEEK: #30

DATES: May

DAY	WORKOUT	COMMENTS
M	AM—5 to 7 miles PM—45-minute varied Fartlek run	
Tu	AM—Light run PM—(1) 3 x ¾ (62's) 　　(2) Easy run 　　(3) 9 x 330—3 in 48—3 in 46—3 in 44	
W	AM—7 to 10 miles at comfortable pace PM—7 to 10 miles at steady pace	

Th	AM—7 to 10 miles
	
	PM—(1) 6 x 330 (45)
	      (2) 7 to 10 miles
	      (3) 6 x 330 cut-down	

F	Light run	
Sa	AM—Light run PM—OSU COMPETITION Mile	
Su	Long easy run (Next week 2-mile)	

EVENT:

WEEK: #31

DATES: May

DAY	WORKOUT	COMMENTS
M	AM—5 to 7 miles PM—40-minute varied Fartlek run	
Tu	AM—4 to 6 miles PM—(1) 2 x 440—660—440—220 61.5-62 pace 10-minute grass between sets (2) 10-minute grass (3) 4 x 330 (49-47-45-43)	
W	AM—4 to 7 miles PM—30-minute steady run 2 x 110 (12)	

Th	AM—3 to 6 miles
	
	PM—3 x 330 (46)
	    2 x 220 (29-28)
	    1 x 110 (12)
		Travel for Pac-8
		Championships.

F	AM—Light run PM—Light run	
Sa	AM—Light grass run PM—COMPETITION 3 Mile	Pac-8 Championships.
Su	Travel—Long, easy run at home	

EVENT:

WEEK: #32

DATES: May

DAY	WORKOUT	COMMENTS
M	AM—5 to 7 miles PM—45-minute varied Fartlek run	
Tu	AM—30-minute run PM—(1) 6 x 440 (48) (220 rest) (2) 30-minute run	
W	AM—4 to 7 miles PM—4 to 7 miles	

Th	AM—5 to 7 miles PM—(1) 4 miles (75 pace) 　　　(2) 3 x 330 (49-46-43)	
F	AM—Light run PM—Light run	
Sa	10 AM (1) 4 x ¾ mile (goal pace for 3 miles) (2) 3 x mile (70—68—66) PM—Light run	
Su	12 to 15 miles easy	

EVENT:

WEEK: #33

DATES: May

DAY	WORKOUT	COMMENTS
M	AM—4 to 7 miles PM—45-minute varied Fartlek run	
Tu	AM—4 to 7 miles PM—(1) 440—660—440—220 (goal pace for mile) 　　　(2) Light grass run	
W	AM—5 to 7 miles PM—5 to 7 miles	

Th	AM—Light run PM—TWILIGHT COMPETITION 2-Mile	
F	AM—Light run PM—Light run	
Sa	10 AM (1) 5 miles at 80 pace (2) Light grass PM—20-minute grass run	
Su	Travel to NCAA Site 12-mile run at comfortable pace	

EVENT:

WEEK: #34

DATES: June

DAY	WORKOUT	COMMENTS
M	AM—Light grass run 11 AM (1) Mile grass run (2) 2 x 330—accelerate—float—accelerate PM—Light grass run	
Tu	AM—5-mile grass run PM—(1) 6 x 330 (47) 　　　(2) 20-minute grass run 　　　(3) 3 x 220 (31-29-27)	
W	AM—Light grass run PM—Light grass run	

Th	AM—Light grass run PM—Preliminaries for NCAA 5,000	
F	PM—Light grass run	
Sa	AM—Light grass run PM—Finals NCAA 5,000	
Su	Travel home Light grass	

EVENT: Preparations for the 1972 Olympics

WEEK:

DATES: July 1972

DAY	WORKOUT	COMMENTS
Sa **15**	330's—Change of Pace	
Su **16**	12-mile steady run	
M **17**	AM—9 x 330 PM—(1) 5 to 7 miles (2) 4 x 110 (15-14-13-12)	

Tu **18**	AM—Light run PM—Light run	
W **19**	(1) 6 x 880 (66.61) (2) 9 x 330	
Th **20**	Travel—Light run (if possible)	
F **21**	Light run	

EVENT:

WEEK:

DATES: July 1972

DAY	WORKOUT	COMMENTS
Sa **22**	AM—5-mile run PM—12 x 330 (48-43)	
Su **23**	8 to 15 miles steady	
M **24**	Light run	

Tu **25**	(1) 3 x ¾ (65-63-61) (880 rest)
	(2) 9 x 330—3-48
	                 3-45
	                 3-42	

W **26**	Light run	
Th **27**	Light run	
F **28**	8 to 12 x 330	

EVENT:

WEEK:

DATES: July/August 1972

DAY	WORKOUT	COMMENTS
Sa **29**	2 x 220 (24-25) Easy run—4 x 110 (14-13-12-12)	
Su **30**	10 to 12 miles	
M **31**	Light run	

Tu **1**	Light run	
W **2**	COMPETITION 3,000 meters	
Th **3**	COMPETITION 3,000 meters	
F **4**	Light run	

EVENT:

WEEK:

DATES: August 1972

DAY	WORKOUT	COMMENTS
Sa **5**	(1) 12 laps (63-80 drill) (2) 3 to 5 miles (3) 6 x 110 cut-down	
Su **6**	Light run	
M **7**	Light run	

Tu **8**	Light run	

W **9**	(1) 12 x 440 (62-66) (110 rest)
	(2) 3 miles at 6:00
	(3) 9 x 330—3-49
	             3-46
	             3-43	

Th **10**	Light run	
F **11**	Light run	

EVENT:

WEEK:

DATES: August 1972

DAY	WORKOUT	COMMENTS
Sa **12**	(1) 3 x mile—4:24; 4:20; 4:16 (880 rest) (2) Light run (3) 6 x 330 cut-down	
Su **13**	Light run in woods	
M **14**	Light run	

Tu **15**	AM—Run 8 x 330 (easy—medium hard) Light jog PM—(1) 6 x 330 (42-45) (2) Light run	
W **16**	Light run	
Th **17**	(1) Mile—61-62 (2) Light run (3) 4 x 660 (70)—440 (65)—330 (47)—220 (30)—110 (13)	
F **18**	Light run	

WEEK:

DATES: August 1972

DAY	WORKOUT	COMMENTS
Sa **19**	10 AM 6 x 330 (43-45) 6 to 10 miles 6 x 330 cut-down PM—Light Fartlek	
Su **20**	12-mile run in woods or trails	
M **21**	Light runs	

Tu **22**	(1) 2 x 6 laps 80-80-70-70-60-60 or 3 miles of 30-40 (2) Light run (3) 3 x 330—220—110 cut-down	
W **23**	Light grass	
Th **24**	2 x 165—9/10—Light run—4 x 110—14-14 12-12	
F **25**	Light grass	

EVENT:

WEEK:

DATES: August 1972

DAY	WORKOUT	COMMENTS
Sa **26**	4 miles at 70-75 pace—4 x 110 (15-14-13-12)	
Su **27**	Light grass	
M **28**	Light grass	

Tu **29**	(1) 4 x ¾—66
	          65
	          64
	    64-63-60
	(2) 3 miles easy
	(3) 6 x 330 cut-down	

W **30**	Light grass	
Th **31**	Light grass	

EVENT:

WEEK:

DATES: September 1972

DAY	WORKOUT	COMMENTS
F **1**	6 x 330 (48)—5-mile run—6 x 330 cut-down	
Sa **2**	Light grass	
Su **3**	Light grass	

M 4	4 x 165 (21)—3 miles easy—4 x 110 (15-14-13-12)	
Tu 5	Light grass	
W 6	5,000 Preliminaries	
Th 7	Light grass	

EVENT:

WEEK:

DATES:

DAY	WORKOUT	COMMENTS
F **8**	Light grass	
Sa **9**	5,000 Finals	

Steve Prefontaine

chapter six

the health of the runner

Runners aren't born hypochondriacs. Yet, being free of injuries and staying healthy is of constant concern to all runners and their coaches.

Many words have been written about the records of Steve Prefontaine. But one of his most unique records has been overlooked: In his four years of training and competing as an undergraduate at the University of Oregon, he never missed one day of training or one competition because of illness or injury! Certainly Pre was a rare specimen. But beyond this, I believe his durability and consistent good health stemmed from the steps taken at Oregon to help prevent injuries and illnesses. These are the guidelines to good running health followed by Prefontaine and all Oregon runners.

PROPER RUNNING TECHNIQUE

Correct technique could have been included earlier as one of the principles of running. But I think it's more relevant to this section, because a majority of the injuries of the foot, ankle, leg, knee, and hip are a direct result of improper running technique.

Overstriding and running on the ball of the foot create most of the problems. The runner whose foot strike is on the ball of his foot rather than the heel could cause himself to get a case of shin splints or stress fractures of the foot. It is much easier to teach someone to run correctly with a heel-ball landing of the foot at the beginning than it is to get someone to adapt to this style after a few years of incorrect technique. Anyone who finds it impossible to correct an improper technique should—for his own protection—seek out soft surfaces as much as feasible for training. He should train in a shoe that has a well-cushioned sole covering the ball of the foot.

To prevent shin splints a runner should daily stretch the muscles in the front of the foreleg. From a sitting position, chair or bed, cross one leg over the other. Then use your hands to work the foot around in all positions, forcing it beyond its normal range of motion to achieve maximum stretching of these muscles. One minute daily on each foot could prevent a case of shinsplints that could hamper training for a prolonged time.

In distance running one must conserve all the energy possible. The concern is efficiency in all necessary movement. Overstriding is one of the extremes of inefficiency. Of equal concern is the likelihood that overstriding eventually will lead to knee and hip problems. How many times have you heard someone urge, "lengthen your stride to pick up the pace"? When a runner overstrides, the center of gravity of his body is between the two legs, forcing him to produce extra effort to pull this unbalanced weight back up and over for the next stride. Each time the foot strikes the ground the center of gravity of your body should be directly above the foot strike. The longer the race or training session, the more important this becomes. Overstriding can be

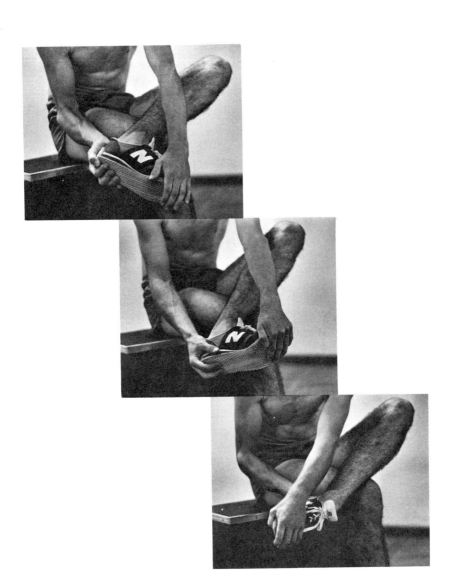

The foreleg muscles are stretched when the runner forces his foot beyond its normal range of motion. This exercise is useful in preventing shin splints.

Rudy Chapa's foot
lands directly
under his center
of gravity.

corrected (once detected) by constantly reminding oneself to
concentrate on a shorter stride. Many times I have made a
runner who is overstriding run behind (just to the outside) of a
runner using correct technique; this forces the overstrider to
shorten his stride.

If you want to pick up the pace, shorten your stride and
quicken your leg speed. Don't reach out further!

The arms are important for balance and rhythm. Quickening

These Oregon runners show good arm position.

the arm tempo increases leg speed. A long pendulum swing of the arms will increase stride length and will result in overstriding. I teach our runners to have a rhythmic action of the arms across the chest approximately sternum high. Try to keep the arms from swinging individually with the elbows going behind the body. In a practice situation this action can be achieved by holding a 6- to 12-inch string between the hands.

Posture and hip position also are important in preventing injuries and developing an efficient stride. Run with an attitude of "running tall." Lift the rib cage and run as vertically as possible to help achieve this feeling. The pelvis should be tilted up for efficiency of leg movement. Develop this stance by standing against a wall, tightening your abdominal muscles, and touching the small of your back against the wall. The pelvis must tilt up to accomplish this. Ever notice the well-developed and clearly defined abdominal muscles of a distance runner? This is a valuable by-product of holding the pelvis in the correct position while running. Sagging of the abdominal muscles will result in an improper tilt of the pelvis, which will put pressure on the lower back region and eventually lead to lower back problems.

The emphasis is on keeping the small of the back tight against the floor in this exercise, which develops abdominal strength for correct pelvic positioning.

A good exercise for development and correct positioning of the pelvis to strengthen weak abdominal muscles is to lie on your back and force the small of the back against the floor by tightening the "abdominals." Slowly lift the legs, together, off the floor and hold to a 30 count. Begin by bending the knees when lifting the legs. But your goal should be to eventually go through this drill with legs locked straight.

REST AND DIET

Despite all that has been written about the runner's diet, common sense should prevail in this area. One should eat and drink what he is accustomed to—in moderation. Vitamins should be used if one is not certain of a balanced diet.

The pre-meet meal should be at least five hours before competition and consist of foods easily digested and high in carbohydrates. Personally, I like a bowl of peaches, toast, and tea or coffee.

Rest is most important! An individual on a regular training pattern should arrange his schedule to allow for ten hours of sleep. Consistency is vital. I encourage my runners to take an afternoon or morning nap when possible. What you do the night before competition seldom influences your performance as much as the cumulative effect of your habits throughout the year.

STRETCHING ROUTINES

Fifteen years ago, few runners bothered to take the time for stretching routines. But the increased mileage involved in modern training programs has made these routines a necessity!

Achilles tendonitis ranks No. I on the list of runners' injuries. As a runner grows older he naturally loses the elasticity of the tendons, compounding this problem. Chronic Achilles tendonitis can severely hamper a training routine; it has ended some promising running careers.

To prevent (or to treat) this problem, I suggest the use of an incline board. The incline board technique involves a static stretch of the Achilles tendon heel cord and the calf muscles.

Materials you'll need to construct your incline board include a ½-inch to ¾-inch sheet of plywood, nails, hammer, saw, tape measure, and some two-by-fours. The basic design is seen in the diagram. Make variations in length and width to suit your needs. The board can be small, or large enough to accommodate several athletes. An angle greater than 30° to 35° is too steep to

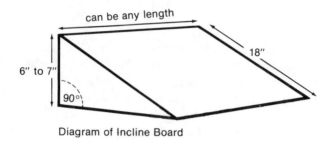

Diagram of Incline Board

be useful. Normally, a height of six to eight inches at the tallest edge will ensure an angle of between 20° to 35°.

The beginning position will depend on the flexibility you have at the talar (ankle) joint. Athletes who are basically inflexible or have tight heel cords should start with the lower end of the board next to the wall as in Position #1. Start at about the middle of the board with your back against the wall. Gradually move your heels down the board, and try to move them all the way to the lower border of the board. If you can get this far with your legs straight and not feel tightness in your calves while the heels are in contact with the board, you should start in Position #2. If this position produces tightness in the calves, it should be your starting point.

In Position #2 the board is turned so that the highest edge is about six inches from the wall and faces the wall. Stand approximately two inches from this top edge and lean in toward the wall. The heels should remain in contact with the board and the legs should initially be straight. This should produce a tightness in the calves of both legs.

The exercise routine consists of two 10-minute periods. If the calf region is tight, the first period is directed to the Achilles tendon area. You will find that by bending or flexing the knees, the stretch is transferred to the Achilles tendon area. You should spend ten minutes in a static (*not* ballistic) stretch of the Achilles tendon. Heels are in contact with the board, knees are bent, and hips are moved toward the wall and kept at maximum stretch for the full ten minutes.

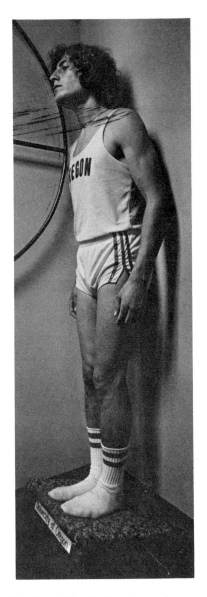 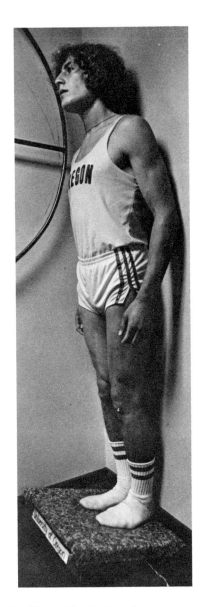

Position #1—incline board. Position #2—incline board.

Final steps in stretching, using the second position
of the incline board.

The second 10-minute period is devoted to the calf muscles. Simply by straightening the legs into full tension you will transfer the stretch back into the muscles of the calf. Keep your heels in contact with the board, knees straight, and hips moved toward the wall.

The stretching period should be a minimum of ten minutes up to a maximum of thirty minutes. Each time the board is used, try to move further down the board so that the angle at the ankle joint is each day (or week) decreased, while the calf muscles and tendons are stretched to the maximum. Try to make your downward movements in increments of one to two inches.

If you use the incline board after an injury, let your pain be your guide. When you reach a point of pain, back off to a less demanding level of stress.

Some suggestions on the use of the incline board follow:

Don't wait for an injury.

When you start, stay with it. Be consistent.

Bring some reading material.

Carpet the board for comfort.

Take your shoes off when using the incline board.

Get accustomed to using the board both before and after runs.

WEIGHT TRAINING

Weight training is included in this chapter because I feel it correlates closely with one's well-being.

In our weight program for runners, an attempt is made to include exercises that require a full range of motion for maximum flexibility and strength of the joint and limb. Other areas being equal, the runner with the greater strength has to have the advantage. Also, he should be less injury prone.

A basic program is presented for your consideration. This program is altered within our own program to meet the varying needs of the individual runners. If used, it should be adapted to meet your needs!

COMMENT— RUNNER'S WEIGHT ROUTINE

EXERCISE	SETS	REPS	DAYS	COMMENT— RUNNER'S WEIGHT ROUTINE
Dumbbell Flys	1	25	M-W-F	10 lb. weights
Leg Press	3	50	W	Add weight each month
Breathing Dead Lift	3	10	M-W-F	As heavy as you can position
Seated Press	3	8	W	Start with ¼ body weight
Bench Press	3	8	M	Start with ¼ body weight
Pull Downs	3	8	F	
Rope Climb	2		M-W-F	Build up to no legs
Sit-ups	4	25	M-W-F	
Straight Arm Pullovers	3	8	W-F	Bar only increase monthly to 40 lbs.

Winning as an individual; winning as a team.

EQUIPMENT

The clothing and shoes you train and compete in influence your well-being. While training facilities and methods have made great improvements, running apparel has kept pace!

Your shoes are your contact with the ground, so they have priority. Look for training shoes that will give good arch support, heel lift, Achilles protection, and comfort. Weight is not as essential as comfort for training. For competition, shoe weight becomes important.

For clothing, look for lightness plus warmth. Clothing should be loose enough so it won't bind, yet not baggy.

COMMONSENSE ATTITUDES TOWARD ILLNESS AND INJURY

The highly trained runner is like a finely tuned engine. It does not take much to throw him off!

In peaking for a performance, avoid unfamiliar activities. Don't try to train "through" an injury. Most likely it would result in additional injuries. Rest is the best treatment for most running related injuries. When you can walk and then jog without favoring the injury, training may begin. Don't rush to make up what you lost, but progress from where you are.

The common cold takes ten days to run its course. If you insist on hard training through this period, you can bring on secondary infections that may set you back additional days.

Learn to "read" and understand your body. When run-down or tired, cut back on workouts. Do not continue to tear down. Occasionally, a two-to three-day layoff can be of great benefit.

Running at your best requires a lot of hard work, a good running program that fits *you,* common sense, and a certain amount of good luck.

Good luck!

index